NOW YOU KNOW EVERYTHING ALMOSTING

The Book of Answers
VOL. III

Doug Lennox

THE DUNDURN GROUP

TORONTO

Editors: Kate Pedersen and Andrea Pruss
Illustrations: Catriona Wight
Design: Jennifer Scott
Printer: Webcom

Library and Archives Canada Cataloguing in Publication

Lennox, Doug
  Now you know : the book of answers / Doug Lennox.

Vol. 2 has title: Now you know more : the book of answers; vol. 3.
  has title: Now you know almost everything.
ISBN 1-55002-461-2 (v. 1).--ISBN 1-55002-530-9 (v. 2).--ISBN 1-55002-575-9 (v. 3)

  1. Questions and answers. 2. Curiosities and wonders.
I. Title. II. Title: Now you know more. III. Title: Now you know almost everything.

AG195.L45 2003   031.02   C2003-903531-X

1   2   3   4   5   09   08   07   06   05

Conseil des Arts
du Canada

Canada Council
for the Arts

Canadä

ONTARIO ARTS COUNCIL
CONSEIL DES ARTS DE L'ONTARIO

We acknowledge the support of the **Canada Council for the Arts** and the **Ontario Arts Council** for our publishing program. We also acknowledge the financial support of the **Government of Canada** through the **Book Publishing Industry Development Program** and **The Association for the Export of Canadian Books**, and the **Government of Ontario** through the **Ontario Book Publishers Tax Credit** program, and the **Ontario Media Development Corporation.**

Care has been taken to trace the ownership of copyright material used in this book. The author and the publisher welcome any information enabling them to rectify any references or credit in subsequent editions.
                                                    J. Kirk Howard, President

Printed and bound in Canada.✪
Printed on recycled paper.
www.dundurn.com

Dundurn Press
3 Church Street, Suite 500
Toronto, Ontario, Canada
M5E 1M2

Gazelle Book Services Limited
White Cross Mills
Hightown, Lancaster, England
LA1 4X5

Dundurn Press
2250 Military Road
Tonawanda NY
U.S.A. 14150

ALSO BY DOUG LENNOX

Now You Know
ISBN: 1-55002-461-2 • $19.99, £10.99

Now You Know More
ISBN: 1-55002-530-9 • $19.99, £10.99

This book is dedicated to "Sprout," aka Jordan

If you have to wonder whether what you're doing is right or wrong
... it's probably wrong.
D.L.

ACKNOWLEDGEMENTS

Everyone needs encouragement, and for me it comes from a myriad of mentors and good people, including Jean-Marie Heimrath, Gerry Jordan, Jonathan and Tom, and Peter Maheras.

CONTENTS

PREFACE

The phenomenal success of the first two books in what is now a series has encouraged this the third "Book of Answers."

It seems that Canadians are fascinated with why we say certain things, how customs and everyday rituals and language originated, and the history behind this evolution.

For the thousands who now own *Now You Know* and *Now You Know More*, *Now You Know Almost Everything* continues with the same formula of dispensing knowledge concisely, never losing sight of the joy and fun of discovering the "why" of ordinary things.

Researching these books has been a delight, and each "nugget" I discover is collected with the enthusiasm of a prospector, anxious to share with you the results of my "digging," so I thank you for educating me. What I have learned, beyond the facts in these books, is that the consequences of history are alive within each of us. Soldiers came back from distant and ancient wars with new expressions and customs that we now use without question. Terms coined by pirates and sailors on the high seas still enrich our daily lives, and we continue to see life and death or games of chance with the same wonder as the ordinary citizens of the ancient civilizations of Greece and Rome or India and China, and within our common pursuit of understanding, we still express ourselves in their words and rituals.

The silent discovery of this research confirms, at least to me, that life on this small planet is a common experience. There is comfort in realizing that borders are illusions of ambitious men and that time has no concern — and maybe even disdain — for the bullies or conquerors; the natural order of things continues at its own pace, like the rising or setting of the sun.

Each of these volumes has its own character, and even though they fall under the general umbrella of trivia, the concise information contained in each subject has clues that could lead to an individual's pursuit of more detail if he or she wished. Aside from my main purpose of entertainment, I have kept in mind that readers, especially children, might be intrigued enough by the answers to do some exploring of their own. To this end, and to add spice, in this volume, after a few of the topics that asked for expansion, I have added points of extra information.

This then is a continuation of our shared learning that the answer to everything is just beyond the obvious. It fascinates me and so, I assume, it does the reader. I remind you that this third collection, although thoroughly researched, is intended as fun.

Although the title *Now You Know Almost Everything* is a smiling reference to all three books, I assure you that there is always more to learn, and besides, I have to keep something to myself. Enjoy!

CUSTOMS

Why is marriage called "wedlock"?

Wedd is an Anglo-Saxon word meaning "to gamble," and there is no greater gamble than marriage. In the days when brides were bartered by their fathers, and a deal was reached with a prospective groom through an exchange of either property or cash, a young woman would have been bought and sold for breeding purposes to be finalized in a wedlock ritual called a wedding. This marriage led to *matrimony*, which in Latin means "the state of motherhood."

Why is it bad luck for the groom to see his bride before the ceremony on their wedding day?

It's bad luck for the groom to see the bride within twenty-four hours of the wedding ceremony for the same reason that brides wear veils. When marriages were arranged by two families, the groom wasn't allowed to see or even meet his bride until he lifted her veil *after* they were married. This way, he couldn't refuse to marry her if he didn't like her looks. The twenty-four-hour ban descends from that ritual.

How did wedding cakes become so elaborate?

Most wedding rituals are to encourage fertility, and so it is with the wedding cake, which began with the Romans breaking small cakes of wheat and barley over the bride's head. During the reign of Charles II, the three-tier cake with white icing we use today was introduced. The cake takes its shape from the spire of Saint Bride's Church in London. The couple cuts the first piece together as a gesture of their shared future, whatever it might bring.

Why do women cry at weddings?

Men might cry at weddings, but they have been socially conditioned that as protectors and warriors signs of weakness such as tears invite an attack. There is no such thing as "happy" crying. Psychologists suggest

that when people cry at happy endings, they are reacting to the moment when the critical outcome was in doubt. A woman crying at a wedding is most likely expressing subconscious disappointment in the outcome of her own romantic dreams.

Why does the groom crush a glass with his foot at a Jewish wedding?

Near the end of a Jewish wedding ceremony, after the vows have been made, wine is poured into a new glass and a blessing is recited over it by the rabbi. After the couple drinks from the glass, it is placed on the ground and crushed by the groom's foot. This symbolizes the destruction of the Holy Temple in Israel and reminds guests that love is fragile. Those gathered shout "mazel tov," and the couple kisses.

Why do Jews place stones on a grave when they visit a cemetery?

At the end of the movie *Schindler's List*, the cast and some of the survivors visit the graves of those whom Schindler worked with and each places a stone on the headstone, where Christians customarily place flowers. This ancient Jewish custom dates back to Biblical times, when stones adorned graves as markers. Today the stones reflect the importance of each soul and are a permanent record of all the people who come to pay their respects.

What is the difference between a parlour and a drawing room?

If you are invited to a stately home for dinner, you are first directed into the parlour, where, through introductions and conversation, you mingle and become acquainted with your host and other guests. It's called a parlour after the French word *parler*, meaning "to talk." After the meal, you retire to the drawing room for liqueurs and cigars. The name "drawing room" is an abbreviation of "withdrawing room" and was originally for men only.

What are the subtleties hidden in the Japanese custom of bowing?

A Westerner probably won't notice the sophisticated use of the bow in Japanese culture. There are four bows, each with a different meaning. The simplest, at an angle of five degrees, means "good day." A bow of fifteen degrees is more formal and means "good morning." As an appreciation of a kind gesture the angle is thirty degrees, while the most extreme, a bow of forty-five degrees, conveys deep respect or an apology. During a recent five-year period, twenty-four residents of Tokyo died while bowing to each other.

What's the difference between an epitaph and a cenotaph?

We gather at the cenotaph on Remembrance Day because a cenotaph is a monument inscribed to honour the dead but which does not contain any remains. An epitaph is inscribed on the tombstone above a grave. Both words and concepts are Greek in origin. Today, the simplest epitaphs are for Catholic clergy: seven crosses for a bishop, five for a priest, and one for parishioners.

What is the origin and meaning of the Latin male gesture of kissing the fingertips?

Latinos and Europeans use hand gestures differently than North Americans. Kissing one's fingertips before directing them toward the object of esteem can be an appreciation of anything from a good wine to a good soccer play. It simply means something is beautiful. The custom comes from the Romans, who kissed their fingertips and then directed them to the gods when entering or leaving a temple.

Why does the audience stand during the Hallelujah Chorus?

In 1741, after Handel introduced his majestic *Messiah*, demand was so great that in order to increase seating gentlemen were asked to leave their swords at home and women were asked to not wear hoops. When England's King George II first heard the Hallelujah Chorus he rose to his feet in awe, and the entire audience followed. From that day on, it's been tradition to stand during the final movement of the *Messiah*.

George Frideric Handel was inspired to compose the entire *Messiah* in just twenty-three days.

BELIEFS
&
SUPERSTITIONS

What's the origin of the parting wish "Godspeed"?

The word *Godspeed* has nothing to do with haste. The archaic meaning of the word *speed*, as used in this case, meant *succeed* or *prosper*. Just as *goodbye* came from "God be with you," *Godspeed* is an abbreviation of "May God speed you" and was first heard in the late fifteenth century. A modern translation might be "May God grant you success."

Why do we say that someone who's finished or fired has "had the biscuit"?

If someone has "had the biscuit," they're definitely done, regardless of the circumstances. The expression has its origins in a Protestant allusion to the Roman Catholic sacrament of Extreme Unction. *Biscuit* is a contemptuous reference to the host (the sacramental wafer used by Catholics during the issuing of the last rites to a dying person). If he's "had the biscuit," it's all over.

Where did we get the expression "For the love of Pete"?

This phrase and others like it (for example "For Pete's sake") are euphemisms for the phrases "For the love of God/Christ" or "For God's/ Christ's sake" and hail from a time when those phases were considered blasphemous. Nowadays phrases like "For the love of God" are commonly used, but the euphemisms are still used as well. Why Pete? Most likely it is a reference to the catholic Saint Peter.

Other phrases with similar origins are "Zounds" (archaic British slang), a contraction of "Christ's wounds"; "Oh my goodness" and "Oh my gosh" for "Oh my God; and "Gosh darn it" for "God damn it."

Why shouldn't you say, "holy mackerel," "holy smokes," or "holy cow"?

As innocent as it seems today, "holy mackerel" began as a blasphemous Protestant oath against the Friday fish-eating habit of Catholics. The fish was an early symbol of Christianity. Likewise, "holy smokes" is a snide reference to religious incense burning, while "holy cow" is a shot at Hindus who consider cows sacred. "Holy moley" is an abbreviation of "holy Moses."

Euphemisms are used as curses without direct reference to a religious icon. Even though it is clear what they mean, it is a way of swearing without offending the pious.

How did Pat Robertson's television show *The 700 Club* get its name?

Today, Pat Robertson's Christian Broadcasting Network is a multi-million-dollar conglomerate, but when they first went on the air in 1961, Robertson's refusal to seek commercial revenue meant that only prayer and telethons kept them going. At the time, Robertson told his audience that a club of seven hundred viewers contributing ten dollars each per month would pay expenses. The success of Robertson's effort gave *The 700 Club* its name.

Why do most flags of Islamic countries have the same basic colours, and what is the symbolism of the crescent moon and star?

The Turkish city of Byzantium was dedicated to the goddess Diana, whose symbol was the crescent moon. In 330 A.D., Constantine rededicated the city to the Virgin Mary and added her symbol, the star. The symbol was common on the arm of Christian soldiers, including Richard I. When Muslims captured the city in 1453, they reconfigured the two symbols and added their own religious significance — the crescent moon and star of Islam represent a conjunction of the moon and Venus during the dawn of July 23, 610, when the Prophet Mohammed (peace be upon him) received his first revelation from God. Mohammed carried two flags into battle: one was green, while the other was black with a white outline, the same basic colours of Islam to this day.

Byzantium became Constantinople before becoming modern-day Istanbul.

The Star and Crescent was first hoisted as a Muslim symbol by Mohammed II in 1453.

Christians dropped the symbol when it became prominent among Muslims.

What is the Holy Grail?

Today we often refer to anything elusive and sought-after as a "Holy Grail" because from the Crusaders to the present, the search for the original Holy Grail has consumed Christendom. The "grail," or bowl, in question was used by Christ at the last supper and disappeared after his crucifixion. Legend has it that the Holy Grail surfaced in England during medieval times and finding it became an obsession of King Arthur.

Part of the legend is that Joseph of Arimathea used the grail to catch the blood of Christ at the crucifixion.

The Old English *greal* is from the Latin word *crater*, meaning "bowl."

Why is unconsummated love called "platonic"?

Greek philosopher Plato observed his teacher Socrates' great but non-sexual love for young men, and concluded that the purest form of love exists only within the mind. Ideal love's perfection is spiritual, and that perfection is often destroyed by a sexual act. Eventually, Plato's philosophy on love was expanded to include women. "Platonic love" entered popular use in English around 1630.

Where else, other than on a Friday, is the number thirteen considered unlucky?

Friday the thirteenth is considered unlucky, but the superstition also applies to apartments, 80 percent of which don't have a thirteenth floor. Airplanes have no thirteenth aisle, and hospitals and hotels have no room number thirteen. The most bizarre superstition is called the Devil's luck, for those with thirteen letters in their names, including

Jack the Ripper, Charles Manson, Jeffrey Dahmer, Theodore Bundy, Albert De Salvo — and Douglas Lennox.

Do people *really* fear Friday the thirteenth?

On Friday, October 13, 1307, the Grand Master and sixty of the Knights Templar were arrested, tortured, and then murdered by King Philip IV of France. Each year, thousands who fear the date fall ill or are injured in accidents. In North America over $900 million is lost in business on Friday the thirteenth because some workers and consumers are afraid to leave the house. Over any given 400-year cycle the thirteenth day of the month occurs 4,800 times. The distribution of thirteenth day of the month is as follows:

Monday, 685 or 14.27 percent
Tuesday, 685 or 14.27 percent
Wednesday, 687 or 14.31 percent
Thursday, 684 or 14.25 percent
Friday, 688 or 14.34 percent
Saturday, 684 or 14.25 percent
Sunday, 687 or 14.31 percent

This means the thirteenth day of the month is only slightly more likely to occur on a Friday!

GAMES
&
ENTERTAINMENT

Why is a skin-tight garment called a "leotard"?

Jules Leotard was the inspiration for the song "The Man on the Flying Trapeze." He made his first public appearance in 1859 with the Cirque Napoleon and began a career of trapeze stunts that made him the toast of Europe. Leotard invented a one-piece, skin-tight garment to free his movement and display his physique. The garment made its way into the ballet studios of Paris and was known in English by 1859 as a "leotard."

Leotard called his garment a *maillot*, which now means "bathing suit" in French.

Born in Toulouse, France, Jules Leotard died from smallpox at the age of thirty.

What are the chances of winning one thousand dollars at a casino game of craps?

If a gambler bets one dollar at a time at a craps table, the odds of winning a thousand dollars before losing a thousand dollars are one in two trillion (that's a two with twelve zeros!). If everyone on Earth played this way, betting a dollar at a time until they won or lost one thousand dollars, and then did it over again three hundred times, only one person would ever win, and then only once in all three hundred times.

Why do we judge someone by how they act when "the chips are down"?

Chips are used as a substitute for money in gambling. When things aren't going well a player's pile of chips dwindles until he loses everything or makes a recovery. How he acts under this pressure, "when the chips are down," is an indication of his character. That's how secure, relatively high-yielding stocks came to be called blue chips, because in poker, blue chips are more valuable than white or red ones.

How many five-card hands are possible in a deck of fifty-two, and what is a dead man's hand?

There are 2,598,960 five-card hand possibilities in a fifty-two card deck, which makes the odds of drawing a flush 500 to 1. But in poker there is always fate. Wild Bill Hickok looked like a winner until he was shot in the back while holding two pairs, aces and eights, which is still known as "the dead man's hand."

If its symbol is in the shape of a black clover, why do we call the suit of cards "clubs"?

Playing cards are as old as history, but the suits we use today were introduced to Britain by soldiers returning from the wars of Italy and Spain in the fourteenth century. The Italian and Spanish cards included a suit picturing real clubs, which the French later changed to a trefoil leaf and the English to a clover — but because they had learned the game from the Spanish and Italians, English players continued calling them "clubs."

Card symbols are called "pips."

Card suits in Spain and Italy are coins, cups, swords, and cudgels (clubs).

In Germany they are hearts, leaves, bells, and acorns.

In Switzerland they are shields, roses, bells, and acorns.

What Biblical curiosities are in a deck of cards?

Some people have found religious significance in a deck of cards. To them, the thirteen cards in each suit represent Jesus and the twelve Apostles or Jacob and the twelve tribes of Israel. The jack, king, and queen suggest the Holy Trinity, and when these court cards are removed the remaining forty cards remind them of the numerous references to the number forty in the Bible, including the number of days Jesus fasted and the years the Israelites wandered in the desert.

Other references: Moses was on Mount Sinai for forty days, Jesus preached for forty months and was in the tomb for forty hours,

Jerusalem was destroyed forty years after the Ascension, Elijah travelled forty days before he reached the cave where he had his vision, and Nineveh was given forty days to repent.

What are the names from history of the jacks and queens in a deck of cards?

In a deck of cards the jacks are Hector, prince of Troy; La Hire, comrade-in-arms of Joan of Arc; Ogier, a knight of Charlemagne; and Judas Maccabeus, who led the Jewish rebellion against the Syrians. The queens are Pallas, a warrior goddess; Rachel, Biblical mother of Joseph; Judith, from the book of Judith; and Argine, which is an anagram for *regina*, the Latin word for queen.

Parisian card names by suit:

Spades: (queen) Pallas, (jack) Ogier
Hearts: (queen) Judith, (jack) La Hire
Diamonds: (queen) Rachel, (jack) Hector
Clubs: (queen) Argine, (jack) Judas

The kings in a deck of cards represent which real leaders from history?

The four kings in a deck of cards were designed in fifteenth-century France, and they represent great leaders from history, while the suits signify the cultures they led. Spades honour the Biblical Middle East, and the king is David. Clubs are for Greece, with the king being Alexander the Great. Julius Caesar honours the pre-Christian Roman Empire as the king of diamonds. Finally, hearts recall the Holy Roman Empire, and the king is Charlemagne.

Why are there jokers in a deck of cards?

The joker was introduced to a deck of cards by American sailors and was added to euchre as the "best bower" in around 1870. Euchre is an

Alsatian card game and was spelled "juker," with the J pronounced "you." In English it was spelled as it sounded: "euchre." Eventually, the sailors' translation hardened the J, and "you-ker became "joo-ker" before marrying with "poker," where it became "joker."

The joker isn't included in the Canadian or British forms of euchre.

The word *bower* in "best bower" is related to *boor*, or "fool," which lends itself well to the joker.

Jokers are sometimes a wild card in poker.

The coloured joker outranks the black and white one.

The court jester on the joker card was added in the 1880s, and the backs of the cards were used for advertising.

How many ways can you win on a ninety-number bingo card?

In 1919, Edwin Lowe saw people playing Bean-O at a carnival in Florida, where they put beans on numbered cards for small prizes. He developed this into a game of chance that became a craze. During its development, a friend who shouted "Bingo!" after winning gave Lowe's game its name. On any given ninety-number bingo card, there are approximately 44 million ways to make B-I-N-G-O. According to suppliers, purple is by far the favourite ink colour in dabbers used by bingo players.

What are the origins and military significance of the phrase "Go for broke"?

"Go for broke" came from the world of professional gambling and is over one hundred years old. It means to risk everything, no matter what the outcome. "Go for broke" was the motto of the segregated Japanese-American volunteers of the 442nd Battalion during the Second World War. At first considered enemy aliens, these soldiers fought so well that they became the most decorated unit in American military history.

Why do we say, "Make no bones about it" when stating an absolute fact?

"Make no bones about it" means nothing has been left to chance. The "bones" of the expression refer to gambling dice, which for thousands of years were made of animal bone. The oldest known dice were found in Iraq and date from 3000 BC. Today, to make no bones about their honesty, the dice used in Las Vegas crap games are precisely calibrated and are manufactured to a tolerance of 0.0002 inches (less than one-seventeenth the width of a human hair).

Why do we say that the person in charge "calls the shots"?

"Calling the shots" means being in control or taking responsibility for critical decisions. The expression comes from a form of billiards. In the game of straight pool the person shooting is required to specify both the ball he or she intends to strike and the specific pocket he or she plans to sink it into. In the mid-twentieth century, "calling the shots" moved out of the smoky pool hall and into everyday usage.

Why does coming in "under the wire" mean you've just made it?

To make it "under the wire" means another instant and you'd have been too late. Before modern electronics, stewards posted at the finish line determined the winners of horse races. A reference wire was strung across the track above the finish line to help them see the order of finish — or which nose crossed the line first. The result of a horse race was determined by the order in which the horses passed under the wire.

Why is a gullible shopper called a "mark"?

A "mark" is someone who can easily be taken advantage of and came to us from midway carnival operators (or "carnies") who run games of chance. The word *midway* was first used to describe the outdoor amusements at the 1893 World's Exposition in Chicago. After a carnie found a victim, and before sending him on his way with a cheap prize, the rogue would slap the rube on the back with a dust-covered hand, marking him as a sucker for operators down the line.

PEOPLE

How many people live on Earth?

On February 25, 2005, the United Nations Population Division issued revised estimates and projected that the world's population will reach 7 billion by 2013 and swell to 9.1 billion in 2050. Most of the growth is expected to take place in developing nations. Nearly all humans currently reside on Earth: 6,411,000,000 inhabitants as of January 2005.

Two humans are presently in orbit around Earth on board the International Space Station. The station crew is replaced with new personnel every six months. During the exchange there are more, and sometimes others are also travelling briefly above the atmosphere.

In total, about four hundred people have been in space as of 2004. Most of them have reported a heightened understanding of the world's value and importance, reverence for human life, and amazement at the Earth's beauty not usually achieved by those living on the surface.

Why does the term *barbarian* refer to a rough or wild person?

The early Greek and Roman term for foreigner was *barbaroi*, meaning that they babbled in a strange language (by which root we also have the word *babble* itself). Another possible contributory origin is the Latin word as *barba* meaning beard. A Roman would visit the *tonsor* to have his beard shaved, and the non-Romans, who frequently wore beards, or *barbas*, were thereby labelled barbarians.

Why do some women wear beauty marks?

Beauty marks highlight facial features, but they began as beauty patches to cover the scars left by a seventeenth-century smallpox epidemic. As the epidemic subsided, women continued using beauty marks as a silent language aimed at potential suitors. One near the mouth signalled a willingness to flirt, one on the right cheek meant she was married, one on the left cheek meant she was engaged, while a beauty mark near the corner of the eye meant, "Let's do it."

How did the expression "barefaced lie" originate?

A "barefaced lie" is one that is obvious and told straight out without flinching by someone who is either very stupid or very brave. The phrase is interchangeable with a "bald-faced lie," in reference to the sixteenth century when most men wore beards, sideburns, and moustaches. Only the rebellious ones who shaved their faces bare were considered bold enough to tell an obvious lie.

Why do some men call a special buddy a "sidekick"?

The slang word *sidekick* describing a close male associate comes from the criminal world and first appeared about 1905. The word referred to the criminal accomplice of a pickpocket. From the mid-nineteenth century, the slang term for men's pants had been *kicks*, and his pockets were on the side of his kicks. The term arose because one man would trip or bump the mark while the other, his "sidekick," would reach into and withdraw cash from the unlucky victim's pocket.

How did street riff-raff get to be called "hooligans"?

In 1898, a London newspaper wrote a series of articles about a gang of street toughs known as "Hooley's Gang" or, as they called themselves, "Hooligans." Strangely, the name also came up in San Francisco and New York about the same time, but because no one named Hooley was ever found it's presumed to be an Irish reference for "rowdy."

Riff-raff means "common" and is from the Anglo-Saxon words for rags (*rief*) and sweepings (*raff*).

Where did the word *tomboy* originate?

A *tomboy* has meant a bold, aggressive girl since about 1579, but before that, a "Tom" was a boisterous, rude boy. If you think of the nighttime habits of a tomcat you might understand that a tomboy, a girl who liked the company of men, was used as late as the 1930s as a reference to a prostitute. This use of the word *tom* is from the Anglo-Saxon word *tumbere*, meaning to dance and tumble around.

Why is a vulgar woman called a "fishwife" while a respectable married woman is a "housewife"?

From its Anglo-Saxon root *wif*, *wife* simply means "woman." A woman's profession, such as a policewoman or chairwoman, often acknowledges her gender in her job title. *Housewife* and *midwife* are among the few titles like this to have survived from medieval times, but at one time, an alewife owned a pub, an oysterwife sold oysters, and a fishwife sold fish. She picked up her vulgarity from the men on the waterfront.

Why are attractive but intellectually challenged women called "bimbos"?

The word *bimbo* is dismissive, and although it generally suggests a dimwitted but attractive woman, it can also be used to describe a stupid or inconsequential man. In some circles, *bimbo* meant promiscuous as well as cute, and it turned up in North America during the 1920s. The word came from within the immigrant Italian community and is a variant of *bambino*, meaning "baby" or "child."

Who were the first people to establish a legal drinking age and why?

In eleventh-century Europe, Asia, and the Middle East, thirteen was the age a person could hold property, drink legally, and, of course, serve in the military. It was the Normans who changed the age to nineteen after realizing that thirteen-year-olds were simply not strong enough for warfare. Today's drinking ages vary from no minimum in China to twenty-one in the United States, but all agree that eighteen is old enough for the military.

Why do we call someone too smart for his or her own good a "smart aleck"?

The expression "smart aleck" for someone too cocky dates back to the 1840s, when New York scam artist Aleck Hoag paid off police to look the other way while he had his wife pose as a prostitute to attract men before breaking in on them, revealing that he was the woman's husband, and demanding money from the frightened man. When Aleck Hoag stopped paying the police, they arrested the couple and coined "smart aleck" as meaning too clever for your own good.

Where did the words *steward* and *stewardess* originate?

A steward or stewardess is usually employed as a caretaker in a variety of circumstances, including at sea and in the air. Although the position carries great responsibility, working conditions are often unpleasant. The title of steward was originally given to someone who took care of the cattle and pigs. It derives from the Anglo-Saxon word *stig-weard*, meaning "sty-keeper." No wonder they want to be called flight attendants.

Why is a perfectionist called a "stickler"?

Stickler is from the Middle English word *stightlen* and means "to arrange." A stickler is a person who does everything by the book. Historically, the stickler was the title of a judge at a duel. Within life and death circumstances he was entrusted to see that the laws of gentlemanly combat were followed to the letter and that the outcome was fair.

Why is a practice session called a "dry run"?

A "dry run" is firefighter jargon. It was once common for firefighters, especially volunteers, to hold public exhibitions of their skills and to compete with other companies at fairs and carnivals. This dry run gave the firefighters practice and was so called because no water was used. A "fire run" or "wet run" is a call to an actual blaze.

Why is a negative perception of someone called a "stigma"?

People held in low esteem are stigmatized for their actions by some outward sign or symbol of weakness. Although *stigma* is a Greek word meaning "puncture," we get the word from the Romans, who called the scar branded on a slave's forehead a stigma. In Hawthorne's *The Scarlet Letter*, the letter A stigmatized Hester Prynne and made a public example of her adultery.

What colour is "Alice Blue"?

President Teddy Roosevelt's sixteen-year-old daughter popularized "Alice Blue." It's a light blue with a hint of gray to match her eyes. During a time of cartwheel hats and the Gibson Girl look, the press nicknamed the pretty young woman "Alice Blue Gown," which became the title of a very popular song written by J. MacCarthy and H. Tierney for their 1919 musical *Irene*. During the 1980s the aircraft carrier USS *Theodore Roosevelt* had many of its prominent areas painted "Alice Blue."

Why is a middleman called a broker?

There are real estate brokers, wedding brokers, pawnbrokers, and, of course, stockbrokers. A broker is someone who arranges or negotiates things. It comes to English from the French wine industry, where *brocour* described the person who bought wine in bulk from the winery and then sold it from the tap. The accepted meaning became anyone who bought something in order to sell it again. In English, the word *brocour* became *broker*, meaning the middleman.

Broker (in its earlier spelling) first appeared in English in 1377 in Piers Plowman: "I haue lent lordes and ladyes my chaffare And ben her brocour after, and boughte it myself."

Why is the person who fixes your pipes called a "plumber"?

A *plumb* or *plumb bob* is the lead weight at the end of a line used to determine the depth of water. It was sailing ships' precursor to sonar. In the fourteenth century, when indoor plumbing was introduced, the pipes were made of lead, and the artisans who installed the pipe systems to buildings took their professional name from what had previously been the metal's main nautical function: they were "plumbers."

SPORTS

Why did it take forty-eight years for a particular Canadian woman to win an Olympic race?

The winner of the women's hundred-metre race at the 1932 Los Angeles Olympics was a Polish athlete named Stanislawa Walasiewicz. The silver medallist was Canadian Hilde Strike. In 1980, when the Polish gold medallist was tragically killed as an innocent bystander during a bank robbery, the ensuing autopsy discovered that *she* was a *he*, and Strike was ultimately declared the winner.

What do the five Olympic rings and their colours represent?

The five Olympic rings were formally introduced in 1920 and represent the union of the five continents or regions of the world that are linked by the Olympic spirit and credo during the Games. The six colours of the Olympic flag, including the rings and white background, are taken from all of the nations' flags. At least one Olympic colour appears on every flag in the world.

In golf, you know about eagles and birdies, but what is an albatross?

Albatross is the Spanish word for "pelican," and although to a mariner it may be bad luck, to a golfer it's an amazing accomplishment. More commonly known today as a double eagle, a three under par for an individual hole was originally called an albatross. Only one has ever been scored in the U.S. Open because the odds of making an albatross are 1 in 5.85 million. Gene Sarazen accomplished this in 1935.

Why are golfers' shortened pants called "plus fours"?

Knickerbockers or knee breeches are pants that only go down to the knee and were quite popular in the first half of the twentieth century. Bobby Jones, among other golfers, found knickerbockers and breeches too restrictive for a full swing. Tailors solved this by designing special golf knickers with an additional four inches below the knee seam, calling them "plus fours." The extra length allowed just enough slack to free up the golfer's swing. Some players wear them to this day.

Where did we get the phrase "Down to the short strokes"?

When a golfer begins at the tee, he hits the ball towards the green by driving, or using a long stroke. When the ball is on the green, he must get the ball in the hole by putting — or taking short strokes. Similarly, a painter (canvases, not houses) begins on a clean canvas using large and broad strokes of the brush. As the painting progresses the brush strokes become shorter and finer as detail is filled into the painting.

Why do we refer to golf courses as "links"?

The word *links* is a Scottish reference to the coastal strips of semi-barren land between the ocean beach and the inland farming areas. Links land was too sandy for crops so it was where the Scots put their first golf courses. There were no trees close to the beach and the sand traps were natural with tall, reedy grass as the only vegetation. Otherwise worthless, these narrow links of land became valuable as golf courses.

Why does the winner of the Indianapolis 500 drink milk in Victory Lane?

After winning the Indianapolis 500 in 1936, Louis Meyer was photographed drinking his favourite beverage, buttermilk. An executive from what is now the American Dairy Association saw the picture in the paper and, realizing it was a good example for children, ensured that from that point on every winner of the Indy 500 would receive a bottle of milk to drink.

How did tennis get its name?

In the eleventh century, French monks started playing a game by batting a crude handball around the monastery. It was a kind of handball with a rope strung across a courtyard. The game progressed and became popular with royalty before catching on in England in the thirteenth century. When returning a ball over the net, the French players shouted, "Tenez," which, roughly translated, means, "Take that!" The English did the same, only "tenez" became "tennis."

What is the origin of the hockey puck?

The origin of the word *puck* is the Celtic game of hurley, where it means "striking the ball with the stick." A "puck-in" after a foul is the act of sending the ball back into play from the sidelines. Since a ball is unmanageable on ice, Nova Scotians and Quebeckers started using a flat wooden puck instead. Their solution was replaced in 1886 in Ontario by a field hockey rubber ball with the top and bottom cut off. Today, a hockey puck is a vulcanized hard-rubber disc, one inch thick, three inches in diameter, and weighing between 5.5 and 6 ounces.

In Ireland, to "puck" someone means to strike him. A puck bird is a robin-sized bird that dives down on goats and strikes them on the back with its beak.

Where did the New Jersey Devils get their name?

The New Jersey Devils began their NHL life as the Kansas City Scouts. Their tenure there lasted only till 1978, when the NHL approved the team's move to Denver as the Colorado Rockies. In 1982 the Rockies relocated once again, this time to New Jersey. After a fan vote, the new team was christened the New Jersey Devils. Most tellers of the legend of the Jersey Devil trace the tale back to Deborah Leeds, a New Jersey woman who was about to give birth to her thirteenth child. The story goes that Mrs. Leeds invoked the Devil during a very difficult and painful labour, and when the baby was born, it grew into a full-grown devil and escaped from the house.

People in the 1700s still believed in witchcraft, and many felt a deformed child was a child of the Devil or that the deformity was a sign that the child had been cursed by God. It may be that Mrs. Leeds gave birth to a child with a birth defect and, given the superstitions of the period, the legend of the Jersey Devil was born.

How did the Boston hockey team get the name "Bruins"?

In the 1920s, Charles Adams held a city-wide contest to name his new Boston hockey team. Because the colours of his Brookside Department Stores were brown and yellow, he insisted that the team wear those same colours. He also wanted the team to be named after an animal known for its strength, agility, ferocity, and cunning. The public contest came up with the Bruins, meaning a large, ferocious bear.

Why is street hockey called "shinny"?

Although shins take a beating during a game of shinny, the name comes from the Celtic game of shinty. A pick-up game of hockey, either on the street or on ice, shinny has no formal rules, and the goals are marked by whatever is handy. The puck can be anything from a ball to a tin can. There's no hoisting, bodychecking, or lifting the puck because no one wears pads. "Shinny" is a uniquely Canadian expression.

The first professional shin pads were hand-stitched leather-covered strips of bamboo, wrapped around the lower leg outside knee-high stockings.

For many Canadian kids during the 1930s and 1940s, copies of the Eaton's catalogue shoved into their socks were their first shin pads.

Why is three of anything called a "hat trick"?

While in Canada it refers to three goals by a single player in a hockey game, a "hat trick" means any accomplishment of three and comes from the English game of cricket. When a bowler retired three consecutive batsmen with three consecutive balls, he was rewarded with a hat. It became hockey jargon during a time when most spectators wore hats, which they tossed onto the rink as a celebration of three goals by one player. During the 1930s and 1940s a local Toronto haberdasher gave any Maple Leaf hockey player a custom-made hat if he scored three consecutive goals.

How did the Detroit Red Wings and the New York Rangers get their names?

In 1932 James Norris purchased the Detroit Falcons hockey team and renamed them the Red Wings. Norris had played for a Montreal team named the Winged Wheelers, which inspired the name and the winged wheel logo on the NHL's motor city franchise. After Madison Square Garden president "Tex" Rickard bought the New York team in 1926, people began calling them after their owner — Tex's Rangers.

How did the stadium phenomenon called "the wave" get started?

"The wave," when crowds at sporting events rise up and down in a continuous pattern, gained its popularity among college crowds during the 1970s and '80s after it was first seen in North America during live telecasts from the 1968 Mexico Olympics. Known in Europe as "the Mexican Wave," the move was revived after it was seen again en masse and on television by fans at the 1986 World Cup of Soccer.

How many teams in the four major North American professional sports leagues have names not ending in the letter S?

There are eight major North American sports franchises whose team names do not end in S, and none of them are in football. They are, in basketball, the Miami Heat, the Utah Jazz, and the Orlando Magic; in baseball, the Boston Red Sox and the Chicago White Sox; and in hockey, the Tampa Bay Lightning, the Minnesota Wild, and the Colorado Avalanche.

How did rhubarb become baseball slang for a fight or argument?

Legendary Brooklyn Dodgers broadcaster Red Barber first used *rhubarb* on-air to describe a baseball altercation in 1943. He said he heard it from reporter Garry Shumacher, who picked it up from another reporter, Tom Meany, who learned it from an unnamed Brooklyn bartender. The anonymous bartender used it to describe an incident in his establishment when a Brooklyn fan shot a Giants fan.

Why don't baseball coaches wear civilian clothes like those in every other sport?

In the 1800s, baseball managers looked after travel and logistics, while a uniformed playing captain guided the team on the field. Captains who had retired from playing kept their uniforms on in case they were needed as a player. Eventually the manager's job expanded to include coaching, but tradition and a 1957 rule insisted that no one without a uniform could enter the playing area, including base coaches and the managers.

During the early twentieth century, the legendary Connie Mack managed the Philadelphia Athletics while wearing a suit and tie and never left the dugout.

What do the record books overlook about the home run records of Hank Aaron, Roger Maris, and Babe Ruth?

Before steroids, Roger Maris's record of sixty-one home runs entered the books with an asterisk because of the longer length of the baseball season by 1961. Babe Ruth hit sixty home runs in 1927 during a shorter season. Most sports fans overlook the fact that Maris broke Ruth's seasonal record with five fewer at-bats, and although Hank Aaron has more lifetime homers than Babe Ruth, the Bambino made almost four thousand fewer trips to the plate.

Roger Maris hit 61 home runs in 1961 with 684 at-bats.

Babe Ruth hit 60 home runs in 1927 with 689 at-bats. He accomplished 714 career home runs over the course of 8,399 at-bats.

Hank Aaron hit 45 home runs in 1962. He batted 755 career home runs over 12,364 at-bats.

Why is someone out of touch said to be "out in left field"?

"Out in left field" means to be misguided or lost, but it generally means to be out of touch with the action. In baseball, left field is generally no more remote then centre or right field, but in Yankee Stadium, when right fielder Babe Ruth was an active player, the choice outfield seats were near the Bambino. Fans in the right field stands derided those "losers" far from the action as being out in left field.

Because Ruth was left-handed, most of his drives went to right field.

Americans and Canadians play the same football game, but why are the rules so different?

In 1874, Montreal's McGill University was invited to play football against Harvard. Harvard was used to playing with a round soccer ball, with different rules than the Canadians, who played rugby using an oblong ball. The game ended in a tie, but the Americans were so impressed with the Canadian game that they adopted the rules. Football as we know it evolved differently on both sides of the border from that game — which ended in a tie.

How did the NFL's Ravens, Bears, and Packers get their names?

The Baltimore Ravens took their name from the classic poem "The Raven" by Baltimore native Edgar Allen Poe. When a football team moved into Wrigley Field in 1921, they took the name Bears to relate themselves to the stadium owner, the Chicago Cubs. The Green Bay Packers are named after the Indian Packing Company, which, in 1919, gave the team $500 for their first uniforms.

How did the Anaheim Angels, the Indiana Pacers, and the Los Angeles Lakers get their names?

The Anaheim Angels took their name from Los Angeles, the city where the franchise began. *Los Angeles* is Spanish for "the angels."

The Indiana Pacers represent the home of the Indianapolis 500, where the pace car leads the field. Although lakes are scarce near Los Angeles, they have a team known as the Lakers because they brought their name with them when they moved from Minneapolis, the land of ten thousand lakes.

How did the New Jersey Nets get their name?

A charter member of the American Basketball Association in 1967, this team was first known as the Americans. When they moved to Commack, New York, a year later they chose the name Nets because nets were an important part of the game, and the name rhymed with other pro teams from New York: the Mets and the Jets.

Why do North Americans call the international game of football "soccer"?

Football goes so far back in history that one form or another has been played by every known civilization. In the 1800s, British football split into rugby and soccer, two games with very different rules. Soccer started out as *socca*, a slang abbreviation of "association" as in "association football," and just like *rugby* became *rugger* through slang, *socca* became *soccer*.

Why are extra seats in a gymnasium or open-air benches in a stadium called "bleachers"?

Bleachers were used in a pinch as uncovered overflow seating from the grandstand before they became common at baseball and football games. The first recorded printed reference was in the *Chicago Tribune* on May 6, 1889. They were called "bleachers" because of their exposure to the sun. The folding seating at an inside gymnasium simply took its name from the open seating outside.

Why is spinning a ball called "putting English on it"?

The expression "putting English" on a ball is used in tennis, golf, soccer, and baseball and means you've spun and curved the ball to overcome a problem. The expression comes from English snooker, a pool game where one of the main strategies is to block an opponent from having a straight line shot at a ball he must hit. To do this, the shooter will create a spin on his shot to circumvent the obstruction. This spin is called "putting English on it."

"Body English" refers to the contortions made by a player as he physically transmits his intention for the ball while it's in motion.

Why is an exercising weight called a "dumbbell"?

A dumbbell is a silent bell devised to strengthen the men who rang very large church bells. At Canterbury in the Middle Ages, it took

twenty-four men to ring one bell. To build up strength (and develop their skills) novices used a silent or "dumb" bell: a heavy weight suspended by a rope from a pulley on a scaffold. People wanting to build up their physiques soon copied with dumbbells of their own.

Why is a sure winner called a "shoo-in"?

The confusion around a shoo-in is in the spelling, which is often written "shoe-in." The shoe isn't footwear. Instead, it's spelled as in *shooing* something to make it move quickly. The term comes from dishonest horse racing when, after conspiring to bet on a probable loser, the jockeys hold back their mounts and urge or "shoo in" a chosen horse through the pack, where it will cross the finish line first and pay off at great odds.

Why is an underdog victory called an "upset"?

The word *upset* means to be unhappy or tipped over. It had nothing to do with sports until August 13, 1919, when, in his seventh race, the great horse Man o' War, who had defeated all of the other greats of his day by fifteen lengths or more, fell victim to an inexperienced starter and lost the race to an unknown competitor named Upset. From then on, *upset* became synonymous with a victorious underdog.

Man o' War retired with a record of twenty wins and only that one loss to Upset. He retired as a three-year-old, lived to be thirty, and became one of the greatest sires in the history of horse racing.

Why do we say that someone who has an advantage has "a leg up"?

If you have "a leg up" on your competition then you're ahead of the game because you've received a boost. The expression comes from the equestrian world. When a rider needs help mounting a large horse, he might ask someone for a leg up. That someone will then create a foothold by cupping both hands so that the rider can use this to step up and get into a position to get his leg up and over the horse's back.

PLACES

Why is Earth the only planet not named from Greek or Roman mythology?

Earth got its name long before the sixteenth century (the time of Copernicus, when humans started considering that we are on just another planet). *Earth* comes from the ancient Germanic languages and originally meant the soil that was the source of all life. Earth is the English name, but hundreds of languages all refer to our fertile soil, our Planet Earth, as a nursing mother. *Terra Mater* means "Mother Earth."

In Roman mythology, the goddess of the Earth was Tellus, the fertile soil.

71 percent of the Earth's surface is covered with water. Earth is the third planet from the sun and the fifth largest.

Why is the city of New Orleans called "The Big Easy"?

It was the jockeys of New Orleans who first began referring to the big-time racetrack in New York as the Big Apple, a phrase popularized by gossip columnist Walter Winchell. Possibly in response to this, during the 1970s New Orleans gossip columnist Betty Guillaud began referring to her city as the Big Easy. The Big Easy was originally the name of a long-forgotten jazz club called the Big Easy Hall.

Why is Boulder City the only city in Nevada where gambling is illegal?

Boulder City was created specifically to house workers from the Hoover Dam building project. Because of the danger and precision of their labour, the government didn't want these men, who earned fifty cents an hour, to be distracted by the consequences of gambling. In 1931, the state of Nevada legalized gambling everywhere except for Boulder City. To this day, Boulder City is gambling free.

The Hoover Dam is 726 feet tall and 660 feet thick at its base. Enough rock was excavated in its construction to build the Great Wall of China.

Who coined the phrase "a New York minute"?

The push for urgency in our day-to-day existence is often expressed as a "New York minute" because that's how long it takes an impatient New Yorker to let you know you're a problem. It was discovered in 1967 as a response to a survey for a Dictionary of American English. One question asked was to fill in the blank after, "I'll be ready in … " to which a Jasper, Texas, policeman wrote "a New York minute."

What are the Seven Seas?

"The Seven Seas" is a figurative reference to all the waters of the world. Rudyard Kipling popularized the phrase for modern times as the title of an 1896 volume of poems. He acknowledged that some would interpret the meaning as the seven oceans — the Arctic, the Antarctic, the North and South Pacific, the North and South Atlantic, and the Indian — but the expression circulated long before these oceans even had names. In the ancient world, the seven seas were the Mediterranean, the Red Sea, the Indian Ocean, the Persian Gulf, the China Sea, and the East and West African seas.

Where did we get the expression "down in the boondocks"?

"The boondocks" refers to an isolated, unsophisticated rural region. Although it's been used in England since 1909, American Marines stationed in the Philippines during the Second World War popularized the term. A *bundok*, in the primary language of the Philippines, is a mountain. The word became entrenched in our language when rediscovered during the 1960s by American soldiers in Vietnam.

What's the difference between the United Kingdom and Great Britain?

The United Kingdom includes England, Scotland, Wales, and Northern Ireland; Southern Ireland is a separate nation. The nations on the large island as well as Northern Ireland share a common government and passport. Great Britain includes the main island of Scotland, Wales, and England and excludes all of Ireland, including the north. It's called Great Britain to distinguish it from Brittany or Little Britain — a province across the Channel in France.

Why is a burial ground for the poor called "Potter's Field"?

Judas Iscariot repented after betraying Jesus and returned the thirty pieces of silver to the conspiring priests. He then took his own life. Because they couldn't return blood money to the temple treasury and Judas couldn't be buried in hallowed ground, the priests used the silver to purchase Jerusalem's Potter's Field, where they buried Judas and gave a name to a burial place for all outcasts.

Why are prestigious hotels and apartment buildings sometimes known as "Arms"?

Some buildings are titled manors or halls and some call themselves arms, like the Windsor Arms in Toronto. The use of the word *arms* is a practice dating back to old English inns, which proudly displayed the coat of arms or heraldic insignia of the local lord above the front entrance. In America, there were no dukes or earls. Instead, they used the word *arms* to convey prestige.

Why do the countries Afghanistan, Kazakhstan, and others all end in "stan"?

The Middle Eastern suffix *stan* is an ancient Farsi word for "homeland." Kazakhstan is from the word *kazakh*, meaning "free," while Kyrgyzstan means "home of forty tribes." Pakistan is an exception. This modern republic took its name from the first letters of Punjab, Afghanistan, and Kashmir, with the suffix *istan* taken from the province of Balochistan. The name *Afghanistan* can be traced to the ninth century Iranian Emperor Apakan.

MONEY
&
NUMBERS

If both the United States and England were $1 billion in debt, which country would owe the most money?

The United States and England calculate both one billion and one trillion differently. One billion in the United States is one thousand million, while in England it is one million million. One trillion in the United States is one million million, while one trillion in England is one billion million. In both cases the British quantity is larger, so if both countries owed $1 billion, England would have the greater debt.

Why is an English pound sterling called a "quid"?

When the people of Great Britain exchange money for goods or services, they will often refer to the value of a pound note as a quid, even though centuries earlier a quid referred to a sovereign, the most important gold coin in history. One pound is equal to one hundred pence. When exchanged for something of equal value the deal in Latin is *quid pro quo* — something for something — which when abbreviated becomes simply *quid*.

Why are subjects of human experiments called "guinea pigs"?

Experimental human guinea pigs are not named after the animal associated with medical testing. Human volunteers selected for observation under trial were usually desperate for money and would receive the nominal daily fee of one guinea for their trouble. A guinea was a forty-shilling piece first minted in 1664, so called because it was minted from West African (Guinea) gold.

The guinea pig animals are misnamed, because they are from Guyana in South America and not Guinea in West Africa.

Why is a differing opinion called "your two cents' worth"?

If someone speaks up out of turn or forcefully inserts their unsolicited opinion, we say he gave his "two cents' worth." The expression dates back to the late nineteenth century, when if you wanted to write an opinion to the editor of a newspaper or complain to a member of the legislature, the cost of mailing the letter was the price of a two-cent stamp. "Two cents' worth" became an Americanism for "of little value."

Why is being called "a lucky stiff" an insult?

If someone wins a lot of money in the lottery and is called "a lucky stiff," it means we think of him as a hard-working, average person who got lucky, but the original meaning of *stiff* described a failure — someone with as much chance of earning that much money on his or her own as a dead person, also called a stiff. A lucky stiff then means that a person (the lottery winner, in this case) is unworthy and undeserving of monetary gain.

If something sounds honest, why do we say it "rings true"?

In the nineteenth century, before the mint started issuing coins with reeding or grooves on the edges to prevent it, some slightly dishonest people would shave the precious metal just enough to go visually undetected. They would then have full value for the coin as well as that of the shavings. If suspicious, a merchant would bounce the coin on a hard surface to hear if it "rang true," thereby proving its authenticity.

The word *ring* is from the Anglo-Saxon *hringan*.

Why are we warned not to take any wooden nickels?

During the nineteenth century, it was common practice at commercial exhibitions to promote the event through wooden coins that could be redeemed at face value only by exhibitors or participating merchants at and during the run of the fair. When the exhibition closed and moved on, patrons were often left with wooden nickels or other coins that were useless unless they could be pawned off to an unsuspecting local retailer.

Why is money called "cash"?

The history of money is fascinating. The word *money* is from the Latin *moneta*, which derives from the Hebrew word *mone*, meaning weight or coins; it is referred to in the Bible as *maneh*. The word *cash* entered English in the late sixteenth century. It's from the French words *casse*, meaning money box, and *cassier*, meaning treasurer, which has given us the word *cashier* and its abbreviation *cash*.

The surname Cash is a variant of Case, and is an occupational name given to persons who made boxes or chests.

Where did the word *dollar* come from?

In 1516, a silver mine opened in the German town of Sankt Joachimsthal in what today is the Czech Republic (St. Joachim was the husband of St. Anne and the father of the Virgin Mary). The German word *thal* means "valley," and the town soon became known simply as Thaler. The silver coins minted from the silver mine were called *thalers*, which by 1600 had translated to English as "dollars" to describe the German coin or any foreign currency.

The Spanish peso was the first foreign currency to be known as a dollar.

Thomas Jefferson resolved that "the money unit of the United States be one dollar" in 1785.

The first American dollar was minted in Philadelphia in 1792.

If gold is so rare, why does there seem to be so much of it in circulation?

Gold is very rare, but it's also very malleable. If, since the beginning of time, all the gold ever mined were to be lumped together, it would make a cube about the size of a tennis court. A cube the size of a matchbox can be flattened into a sheet that would cover that same tennis court, and one tiny ounce of gold can be stretched into a wire fifty miles long. A little gold goes a long way.

What's the difference between yellow and white gold?

Pure or 24-karat gold is yellow and relatively soft. White gold includes an alloy of nickel and palladium. Zinc is added to harden the gold for gem settings. White gold can be more expensive than pure gold because it's harder to fabricate. 18-karat yellow gold is the most popular in Europe and is 75 percent pure gold. 18-karat white gold is 25 percent nickel. 24-karat gold is 99.9 percent pure gold, 22-karat gold is 91.67 percent, and 20-karat gold is 83.33 percent. 20-karat and above is yellow in colour.

In America 14-karat yellow gold is the most popular. 14-karat white gold is harder and yellowish and used in prong settings. It's often plated with rhodium (a form of platinum) to enhance the whiteness.

12-karat gold is 50 percent gold; it is commonly used in class rings and can be a number of colours depending on the added alloy. 10k gold is 41.67 percent gold and is the lowest alloy to be called gold.

Why is the discovery of riches called "the motherlode"?

The expression "Finding the motherlode" is usually used figuratively for the discovery of an abundance of almost anything, but it comes

from the mining camps of the late nineteenth century. A *lode* is a mining term for a vein of metal ore, the discovery of which would be exciting enough, but add "mother" and you've come across the origin of all the veins in the region. The motherlode is, literally, an abundant source of supply.

Why is the furthest we can go called the "nth degree"?

To take something to the "nth degree" means we have exhausted all possibilities. The letter *n* is the mathematical symbol meaning "any number." If you say "nth plus 1" you mean "to the utmost." The expression derives from the mathematical formula *n plus 1* meaning "one more than any number," which of course is beyond the outer limits. The "nth degree" originated as university slang in the nineteenth century.

Why is the last minute before a deadline called "the eleventh hour"?

The reference is to the eleventh hour on the original clock devised by the Babylonians for use with their sundial. The period from dawn to sundown — when a sundial was usable — was divided into twelve hours, so the eleventh hour came just before sunset. In other words, if you did something at the eleventh hour, it was just before you ran out of daylight. You'll find this notion used metaphorically in Matthew 20:1-16, in which we learn that even a sinner can find salvation at the last minute,even someone who procrastinates and doesn't do what he has to do until, well, the eleventh hour.

Why are a group of thirteen things called "a baker's dozen"?

In 1266, the English passed a law regulating the weight and price of beer and bread sold in the marketplace. Bakers depended on middlemen to sell their excess, especially during a good harvest year, but the new law forbade them to offer a discount or a wholesale price. They found a way to skirt the law by adding one extra loaf to each dozen.

This thirteenth loaf provided the profit for the middlemen. The practice of adding the thirteenth loaf is older than the phrase; "a baker's dozen" dates from only 1599.

If you have a myriad of choices, exactly how many choices do you have?

Since the sixteenth century, writers have used the adjective *myriad* to describe a large, unspecified, or overwhelming number, such as, "The student had a myriad of excuses for not turning in his assignment" or "Steve had a myriad of reasons for his wrong decision." Neither of these uses is literally incorrect, but based on its Greek root, one myriad is exactly ten thousand.

Why do they count down backwards to a rocket launch?

After NASA rolls out a rocket they start the countdown at T – 43 (said as T minus 43 hours), and with critical holds, it takes three days before lift-off. The countdown was introduced by German film director Fritz Lang in his 1928 movie *By Rocket to the Moon* and then, much later, copied by real life rocket scientists. Lang introduced the backward count of 5-4-3-2-1 to increase suspense.

How did the numbers eleven, twelve, and thirteen get their names?

The reason the nine numbers after ten are known as eleven, twelve, and the teens is clarified by looking at Roman numerals and considering that they are all plus or minus units of ten and were interpreted into archaic English with this in mind. Eleven (XI) or "leave one" means ten is one less than eleven. Twelve (XII) means ten is two less than twelve. Thirteen is three plus ten (or "teen"), four plus ten is fourteen, and so on.

TRAVEL
&
DISTANCE

What's the difference between a truck, a tractor semi-trailer, and a full tractor-trailer?

Those huge vehicles overwhelming the highways are called tractor semi-trailers because the back portion sits on wheels while the front end is supported by the tractor. A full trailer rides on its own wheels with axles on the front and back and is connected to the tractor by a drawbar. Sometimes a full trailer is attached to a semi, which is attached to the tractor. A truck doesn't have any attachments.

How did the famous Italian automobile brands FIAT and ALFA get their names?

FIAT, or Fabbrica Itailana Automobili Torino, was formed in a 1903 takeover of Ceirano, which had been founded in 1901 to make cars under Renault licence using a deDion engine. Ceirano's assets included a racecar driver named Vincenzo Lancia. In a similar 1910 move, a group of Milanese businessmen took over a factory set up to produce Darracq 4-cylinder taxicabs. This group was called Anonima Lombarda Fabbrica Automobili, or ALFA.

Where did the term "drag racing" originate?

Drag racing is a quarter-mile race between two cars starting side by side from a standing start. It began in the 1950s and was usually held on the main street of a small town. In the nineteenth century, because they were being dragged down the street by a horse, wagons and buggies were called drags, and in the 1850s the name transferred to the main street; it became known as the main drag, which gave drag racing a venue — and its name.

If you're abandoned and alone, why do we say you've been "stranded"?

If you've been stranded, you're abandoned and powerless. *Strand* came to English from the Scandinavians as a word meaning "beach" or "shore," and it now refers specifically to the beach area between the high and low tide. In the seventeenth century, a stranded ship had been beached or left aground on the strand after the tide went out. The general use of the word to describe helplessness dates to 1837.

How far is a league as mentioned in *The Lord of the Rings*?

Folk tales refer to a league as a specific distance. There were seven-league boots, and Jules Verne sent Captain Nemo twenty thousand leagues under the sea. A *league* is an ancient measurement; in medieval England it was simply the distance a person or a horse could walk in one hour, which is about three miles (five kilometres), the same distance as defined by the Romans. The league is no longer an official unit of measurement in any nation.

Why is a country mile considered a greater distance than the average mile?

To "miss by a country mile" means you weren't even as close as if you'd have only missed by a mile. A country mile is an exaggeration of the 1,760 yards in the standardized English distance. Rural roads in Britain twist and turn through the countryside, so although the distance to be travelled is a mile, the real distance travelled on a winding road will be considerably greater than "as the crow flies," or in a straight line.

How long is a "rod"?

The rod is still used as a unit of measurement for portaging in recreational canoeing, possibly because a rod is about the same length as a canoe. A rod was established to be the combined total length of the left feet of the first sixteen men to leave church on Sunday. The distance was standardized in 1607 as 5 yards, or 16.5 feet. An acre is 40 rods by 4 rods, or the area a man and an ox could work in one day.

A rod is the same length as a perch and a pole.

POLITICS
&
THE LAW

Why do Conservatives call Liberals "bleeding hearts"?

The ultra-conservative view of those who propose extending the welfare state is that they are "bleeding hearts." That expression entered politics in the 1930s, and by the 1990s "my heart bleeds for you" had become a general put-down. It comes from the Middle Ages, when a socially conscious group known as the Order of the Bleeding Heart was formed to honour the Virgin Mary, whose "heart was pierced with many sorrows."

Why are Conservatives called "Tories"?

By definition, Liberals want to change things while Conservatives want to maintain the status quo, so it should be no surprise that the word *Tory* is from the Celtic words for "the king's party" and "partisans of the king," both of which were derived from the Irish word *toruigh*, meaning "to ambush." Formed in 1679, the Tory Party became the Conservative Party in 1832, but their opponents continue to call them Tories.

> *Taob-righ* (Celtic for "king's party")
> *Tuath-righ* (Celtic for "partisans of the king")
> *Tar-a-ri* (Celtic for "come o king")

Why is someone you don't want to hear from told to "take a back seat"?

"To take a back seat" means that you have little or no influence in the decisions required to fulfill an objective, and has nothing to do with "back-seat driving." It comes from the parliamentary system of government, where the leaders of all parties — those who make and debate the critical decisions — are seated on the front benches of the House, while those who follow the party line with no input in these matters, other than a vote, take a back seat.

Why are British police officers known as "bobbies"?

In 1828 Sir Robert Peel, then home secretary (and later prime minister), reorganized the London police force into a modern law enforcement agency. Officers in the new department were known at first as "peelers," after their Irish counterparts in a similar reorganization when Peel was secretary for Ireland some years earlier. Bobby is the shortened, familiar form of the proper name Robert. "Peeler" was gradually replaced in the public vernacular by "bobby," and members of the London force are still known as bobbies today.

Why are police vans called "paddy wagons"?

A *paddy wagon* sounds like a logical reference to the great number of Irish policemen in uniform during the late nineteenth century, but not so. "Paddy" is a slur against the common Irish name Patrick, and because the Irish were considered the lowest in the social order, whenever it was politically expedient to appear to crack down on crime, all of the Paddies were profiled and rounded up in police wagons.

How did a broken straw come to stipulate the end of a contract?

Stipulate is from *stipula*, the Latin word for straw, and refers to the specification of an essential part or condition of an agreement. When a landowner in feudal England wanted to remove a serf from his property, he would present the unfortunate tenant with a broken straw symbolizing the termination of their contract. During this time, men of questionable character would loiter around the courthouse offering to testify for money. They stipulated this by wearing a piece of straw in their shoes and were called "straw men."

Why does "pony up" mean "show us your money"?

Gamblers understand that "pony up" means to put your money into the ante to start a poker game or to make good on your losses. *Pone* (pronounced like *pony*) is from the Latin verb *ponere* meaning "to seize," and its current use came from a legal writ of common law instructing a bailiff to seize a defendant's goods or obtain security to ensure his appearance at trial. This writ of pone is more commonly known as bail.

What does it mean to give someone power of attorney?

If you give somebody "power of attorney," that doesn't mean they suddenly become a lawyer; it simply means they can legally sign papers and make decisions for you in the area in which you've given them that power. In many, perhaps most, cases, lawyers are given power of attorney — but it doesn't have to be that way.

The British have several additional terms for people who practise law. *Lawyer* is a general term describing all of them. *Solicitors* do most of the office work, draft documents, talk to clients, and may only appear as advocates in the lower courts. *Barristers* do most of the trial work, especially in the higher courts, where they are the only ones who may act as advocates. *Attorney* has pretty much the same meaning in Britain as in America — one who acts on behalf of another.

What is a "grand jury"?

A grand jury is convened to determine if the prosecution has a case against a criminal suspect. Although still used in the United States, the grand jury has been dropped by Canada and Great Britain because they subvert the presumption of innocence and due process.

Two thirds of all the lawyers in the world live in the United States. Los Angeles has more judges than all of France, while in Washington, D.C., there is one lawyer for every twenty-five men, women, and children.

Why is private property called our "bailiwick," and how does it concern the sheriff?

Bailiwick is an old English legal term and is a compound of *baile*, which is now *bailiff*, and *wic*, meaning a farm or dwelling. From the mid-fifteenth century it's meant "under a bailiff's jurisdiction" — which leads us to the sheriff. During monarchial rule, each English shire had a reeve who acted as chief magistrate for the district. When the title "shire reeve" crossed the Atlantic it became "sheriff."

WAR
&
THE MILITARY

Where did we get the expression "Over the top"?

During the First World War, a charge over the protective battery that ran alongside a trench was called "going over the top." Such a charge usually resulted in many casualties, as did most operations during that tragic conflict. Since the casualty rate was very high, it took remarkable bravery to go over the top. Some considered it excessively brave, and the phrase has come to be associated with excess.

Why do we pronounce *colonel* with an R and spell it with an L?

It's a messy story, the result of confusion between two forms of the word that came into English at different times. Its source is the Italian *colonna*. This (along with the English word *column*, with the same meaning) derives from the Latin *columna*, because a column of men was reminiscent of the shape of a pillar. The Italian *compagna colonnella* (literally, "little-column company") referred to the small company of soldiers that marched at the head of a regiment and was commanded directly by the officer in charge. That officer became known as the *colonnello*. This shifted into French as *coronel*, but later changed back nearer the Italian original as *colonel*. Much the same thing happened in English, where *coronel* was the more common form up to about 1630. For a while after this date both forms were in use until *colonel* eventually won. At first the word was pronounced as three syllables, but the middle became swallowed, and under the continuing influence of the "r" spelling the "l" in the first syllable vanished.

When something is over why do we say, "That's all she wrote"?

"That's all she wrote," meaning "that's the end of it," has a heartbreaking history. During the Second World War, it wasn't uncommon for an overseas serviceman to receive a brief, cutting letter from a girlfriend telling him that their romance was over and that she'd found someone else in his absence. When questioned by his buddies, the anguished soldier's response would be, "That's all she wrote," and it became so common it entered our language as meaning "it's over."

Why do yellow ribbons symbolize fidelity?

Yellow ribbons were first used during the Vietnam War. The inspiration came from a Civil War legend about a soldier returning home from the infamous Andersonville Prison. He had written his wife to hang a yellow handkerchief on the oak tree in the town square if she still loved him; otherwise he would stay on the stagecoach and move on. A modernized version became the hit song "Tie a Yellow Ribbon," and a new custom was born.

L. Russell Brown was inspired to write the song one late spring morning, and he drove thirty-three miles to Irwin Levine's house to tell him the story. Irwin changed the yellow handkerchief to a ribbon so as not to offend anyone with the reality of what makes handkerchiefs yellow. They also updated the story by changing the stagecoach to a bus.

The song was released in February 1973. It was the number one hit by April 1973. The song became a hit again in 1981 when the fifty-two Iran hostages were returned after 444 days of captivity.

Why is a dismissive final remark called "a parting shot"?

In 247 B.C., the warriors of the Parthian Empire were such skilled archers on horseback that even Rome couldn't conquer them. They had developed a saddle with a stirrup, which enabled them to turn and fire arrows while riding away at full gallop. This incredible manoeuvre during a strategic retreat was known as the Parthian shot, which gave us the expression "a parting shot."

The Parthian Empire included, in part, what is now Afghanistan, Pakistan, and most of Iraq and Iran. They took over the region after conquering the Scythians, who had developed the magnificent breed of horse that was the key to the Parthians' success.

While firing arrows, a rider could steady himself with the newly invented stirrups and then guide his mount with his legs.

Why is malicious destruction called "vandalism"?

A vandal mindlessly defaces public property. During the fifth and sixth centuries the Vandals, a Germanic warrior race, expanded south from their Baltic base. They would go beyond defeating their enemies by desecrating their cultural symbols in an effort to humiliate as well as conquer. When in 455 they overwhelmed and then sacked Rome, the Vandals continued to deliberately mutilate public and religious monuments, an act that to this day bears the name "vandalism."

Where do we get the expression "Batten down the hatches"?

"Batten down the hatches" is a traditional naval order to securely cover the openings or hatches to the hold on the deck of a sailing ship. *Batten* is the key word and comes from the same root as the French word *baton*, like the one used by an orchestra conductor or in a relay race. A batten is a strip of wood, which in this case was used to nail down a tarpaulin over the ship's hatches during a storm.

Why do we call an unstable person a "basket case"?

A "basket case" is a derogatory reference to someone considered unstable and has a very sad origin. During the First World War, because some soldiers were so badly maimed or shell-shocked that a stretcher wouldn't hold them, they were carried off the field in wicker baskets. In 1919, after the war, the dark expression "basket case" began being cruelly applied to anyone with an impairment, either physical or mental.

How did crossing a line in the sand become a military challenge?

The concept of a literal "line in the sand" was first created by a lone Roman senator who rode out to meet a Macedonian king at the head of an army poised to invade Egypt, a Roman protectorate. The king balked until the senator drew a circle around him in the sand and demanded that he order a withdrawal before stepping out of that circle or face the wrath of Rome. The king paused and then complied.

This account has been verified by contemporary historians. The senator was Popillius Laenas.

Why is an exact likeness called a "spitting image"?

A boy who looks like his dad is sometimes said to be a spitting image of his father. There is another expression — "spirit and image" — but it isn't related. At the apex of the glory that was the British Empire, just about every man was familiar with the spit and polish discipline of military life. When a man polished his boots, he used saliva to bring them to where he could see his own reflection, and that is the origin of "spitting image."

Why are deadly hidden devices called "booby traps"?

The English word *boob*, meaning "stupid" or "dunce," first appeared in 1599 and comes from the Spanish word *bobo*, also meaning "stupid," which came from the Latin *balbus*. While a booby prize is awarded to the supreme loser, it was during the First World War that the nineteenth-century booby trap changed from being a harmless practical joke to its deadly modern wartime meaning of laying explosive traps for enemy soldiers.

The term "boob tube" refers to television, and is synonymous with "idiot box."

Why is someone of little importance called a "pipsqueak"?

The Allied soldiers came up with the perfect synonym for "non-threatening" during the First World War. The Germans had brutal artillery, but they also had a smaller gun that stood out from the other incoming rounds by its unimpressive squeaking noise. It struck with a sound more like "pip" than "boom." The boys in the trenches called them "pipsqueaks," and after the war, they transferred the meaning as a description of someone of little significance.

Why is there a saddled, riderless horse in a military funeral?

The riderless horse in a military funeral was an ancient custom practised by the Romans. A soldier and his horse trained to fight as one unit in battle, making it almost impossible for the animal to have another master. If a soldier retired, so did his horse. For the same reason, if the soldier died in combat, the horse followed his coffin to the cemetery to be put down and buried with his companion. The two would ride together into the afterlife. The empty boots in the stirrups is a later tradition and signifies that no one else can ride that horse. Today it's simply a ceremony, and the animal isn't harmed.

What's the origin of the panic button?

The first panic buttons were installed in bombers during the Second World War. If his plane was hit by enemy fire, a pilot could push a button that set off an alarm throughout the aircraft. The crew responded with a drill, which, in severe cases and if a crash was imminent, could lead to the entire crew bailing out. When too many chose to parachute when hearing the alarm even though the situation wasn't critical, pilots were advised to think twice before "pushing the panic button."

What does it mean to be decimated?

Around 1663, the word *decimate* began mean being destroyed through a catastrophe or severe loss, but the word originated as a disciplinary practice of the Roman army. Soldiers convicted of cowardice or mutiny were gathered into units of ten. Lots were drawn, and the loser was decimated (clubbed and stoned to death) by the remaining nine. Morale increased significantly after a Roman decimation.

After a decimation, the remaining nine convicted soldiers were given rations of barley instead of wheat and forced to sleep outside of the army encampment.

Although decimation inspired discipline and resolve, it was used sparingly because it significantly reduced troop strength.

How did "diehard" come to mean resilient?

"Diehard" was coined on May 16, 1811, by a British man, Colonel Inglis, who had gathered the men of his 57th Foot Regiment just before the battle of Albuera against Napoleon. The colonel ended his address with, "Die hard my lads, die hard" — and that they did. They were victorious, but only 1 of the 24 officers and 168 of the 584 men survived.

Why do they fire a rifle volley over the grave of a fallen soldier?

Military funerals are filled with traditions, but none as ancient as firing a volley over the deceased. During the Napoleonic Wars, hostilities were ceased to clear the dead from the battlefield. When finished, the detail would fire three shots into the air as a signal that they were ready to resume the fight.

The tradition mirrors the ancient tribal practice of throwing spears into the air to ward off evil spirits hovering over the fallen.

The *caisson* was the wagon used to carry the dead soldiers from the battlefield.

Why do we describe a close contest as "nip and tuck"?

A closely fought contest where the outcome is in doubt is said to be "nip and tuck." It equates to the expression "blow for blow," when the advantage keeps changing from one competitor to another. The answer is in the original aggressive meanings of the two words. A *nip* was (and still is) a bite, while a *tuck* was a small, narrow dagger used by artillerymen when overrun and forced into hand-to-hand combat. "Nip and tuck" literally means a vicious, life and death struggle.

What's the origin of the phrase "Don't shoot the messenger"?

"Don't kill the messenger" was first expressed as long ago as 442 BC by Sophocles. "Kill" became "shoot" in the American West during the nineteenth century. The expression arose during a time when messages between opposing armies, such as terms for surrender, were delivered by hand. The angry reply was often the symbolic return to his own side of the murdered messenger.

FOOD
&
DRINK

Why is someone who is dazed or confused said to be "groggy"?

If you're in a haze you might be groggy, but you're more likely to be drunk because of the grog. Back in 1740, British Admiral E. Vernon changed the drinking habits of his sailors by issuing their rum ration diluted with water and lime juice to prevent scurvy (which is the origin of the label *limey* for an Englishman). The admiral always wore a grogram coat and was known to the men as "Old Grog," which is why the word *grog* is used to describe rum.

A grogram coat is made from a weave of a coarse waterproof fabric (from the French *gros-grain*) made from silk, mohair, and wool and stiffened by gum.

Why is a cup of coffee sometimes called a "cup of joe"?

Up until 1913, the United States Navy practised the British tradition of each sailor receiving a daily ration of rum. But that year, Secretary Joseph (or Joe) Daniels, a non-drinker, prohibited any alcohol on board any American vessel. This made coffee the strongest drink available to the disgruntled sailors, who began referring to their mugs of coffee as a "cup of Joe."

Why did diners name the best bargain of the day a "blue plate special"?

The first fast food restaurants were mobile wagons, and they appeared during the late 1800s. They were called diners because they resembled railroad dining cars. These special cars introduced the blue plate special during the Great Depression of the 1930s after a manufacturer invented a dish with separate, sunken compartments for potatoes, meat, and greens. Disposable and available only in blue, these delicious, quick meals were promoted as the blue plate special.

What is North America's favourite snack food?

North Americans devour 1.2 billion pounds of potato chips each year, making chips our favourite snack food. In 1852 at a resort in Saratoga, New York, Cornelius Vanderbilt sent his French fries back to the kitchen, complaining that they were too thick. Chef George Blum retaliated by cutting new potatoes ridiculously thin, frying them, and sending them back to Vanderbilt — who loved them. Today, a pound of potato chips costs five hundred times more than a pound of potatoes.

93 percent of Americans snack: 50 percent do so two or three times a day, 40 percent four times a day, and 3 percent five or more times a day.

Almost 90 percent of North American households buy potato chips about every three weeks; 76 percent buy tortilla chips once a month.

86 percent of American teenagers eat candy at least once a week.

Why is there a chocolate bar named Sweet Marie?

The Sweet Marie chocolate bar was inspired by a love affair. In 1893, after an evening stroll through the streets of London, Ontario, with his girlfriend Marie, author Cy Warman was so smitten that he sat down in a park and wrote a poem called "Sweet Marie." When musician Raymond Moore read the poem he put it to music, and the song became a hit that inspired a chocolate company to create the Sweet Marie chocolate bar. Cy married his sweet Marie, and together they raised four children in London.

Why do we say that someone we consider stupid "doesn't know which side his bread is buttered on"?

To not know which side your bread is buttered on comes from a Yiddish folk tale describing the stupidity of the men of Chelm in Poland. The story goes that one day, when someone dropped a piece of bread, the wisest men in town gathered to ponder why it landed butter side up. After weeks of deliberation they concluded that the bread had been buttered on the wrong side.

Why are dishes served with spinach called "Florentine"?

When cooked with spinach, Eggs Benedict become Eggs Florentine. When Catherine de Medici of Florence married Henry II of France, she brought with her several master cooks. Soon they were introducing France to new foods such as artichoke hearts, truffles, sweetbreads, and ice cream. When Catherine's cooks served up dishes with the unfamiliar spinach, they were referred to as *à la Florentine*, after the queen's birthplace.

How did an ice cream dish become known as a "sundae," and why is it spelled that way?

In pious New England during the 1880s, the church convinced local councils to ban ice cream sodas on Sunday, because enjoyment of the flavoured treat overshadowed the reverence of the day. The soda

fountains' response was to simply hold back the carbonated soda from the syrup, fruit, nuts, and ice cream and change the name to sundae. The spelling was a clever way to legally promote the dish without referring to the Lord's day.

Why is a small restaurant called a "bistro"?

Legend has it that when the Russian Cossacks occupied Paris in 1815, they were notoriously rude and demanded quick service from local restaurants and bars by shouting what the French understood to be "*Bistro!*" which sounds very much like a Russian word for "quickly." The word *bistro* has no French root, and so the legend is plausible. Regardless, whether French or otherwise, a bistro promises intimate and rapid service.

Where did the expression "Have your cake and eat it too" come from?

Having your cake and eating it too is an idiom meaning that you want to do the impossible by disposing of or consuming something that you want to enjoy, while at the same time keeping it intact. It's an attempt to overcome an either/or situation. It was first written down in 1562 as, "Would you both eat your cake and have your cake?" and somewhere along the line it became, "Have your cake and eat it too."

"Wolde ye bothe eate your cake, and haue your cake?" — *A Dialogue Conteynyng Prouerbes and Epigrammes of 1562* by John Heywood.

"Eat your cake and have it" — 1816 poem "On Fame" by John Keats.

Why do we call outdoor cooking a "barbeque"?

Barbeque is one of the first Native American words to enter our language. The Spanish borrowed *barbacoa* from the Arawak people of the Caribbean. The word described the large wooden frame that the Arawak used either to dry meat or to sleep on. Around 1661, this same framework was found to be excellent for supporting whole animals for cooking over a fire, and the barbecue was born.

How did the caramel-covered popcorn Crackerjack get its name?

Today a "cracker" is someone who breaks into your computer, but among other things, it also once meant something excellent or special. The "Jack" in Crackerjack is the sailor, and the little dog on the package is named Bingo. Trademarked in 1896, Crackerjack got lucky when Jack Norworth included it in his 1908 song "Take Me out to the Ball Game," after which it became part of American culture.

Jack and Bingo didn't appear on the box until 1918, when returning First World War servicemen were very popular.

Jack was a nickname for all sailors.

Where did the drinking expression "Bottoms up" originate?

"Bottoms up" means more than "lift your drink." When press gangs cruised dockside English taverns preying on drunks for naval duty, one of their tricks was to drop a shilling into an unsuspecting target's pewter ale jug. When the drink was empty, the gang would tell him that he had accepted the King's shilling and then drag him off to sea. Wary drinkers began using glass-bottom tankards, and "bottoms up" meant to check for the shilling.

Why are those tasty round pastries with holes in the centre called doughnuts?

In 1809, Washington Irving's *Knickerbockers History of New York* described small, tasty balls of fried dough that, because they resembled walnuts, were called Dough Nuts. The Dutch had introduced them as oil cakes and usually baked them as treats for holidays. After the introduction of baking powder and tin doughnut cutters, the hole was manufactured commercially around 1845.

What does the phrase "Eat, drink, and be merry" tell us?

Today we use "Eat, drink, and be merry" as an invitation to party, but to be merry originally meant to be content or self-satisfied. The phrase is from a parable in the Bible that tells the tale of Epicurious, a man who worked hard all his life to accumulate goods and money and believed that he shouldn't take time to "eat, drink and be merry, for tomorrow we die." When Epicurious died he was remembered as a fool because he did not live for anything but the material. The phrase also appears in Luke 12:19: "Soul, you have so many goods laid up for years to come; take your ease, eat, drink, and be merry."

Why is the word *straw* in *strawberry*?

The Germans call them *erdbeeren* ("earth berries") because they grow on the ground. The Romans called them *fragaria* ("fragrant berries") because of their sweet smell. So how did these delicious treats become known in English as strawberries? It's because the climate of both Britain and Ireland is very damp, and so to grow them, farmers needed to protect emerging berries from the muddy soil. They did this by spreading a layer of straw around each new plant.

Why do we call those tasty sweet treats "candy"?

The sweetness in candy and sugar was called *saccharon* by the Greeks and *saccharum* by the Romans, so it's clear where we get the word *saccharine*. After conquering most of the southern Mediterranean around 1000 AD, the Arabs built the first sugar refinery on the Isle of Crete, which they had renamed *quandi*, meaning "crystallized sugar." In English, *quandi* became *candy*. Caramel was also invented by the Arabs. They called it *kurat al milh*, meaning, "ball of sweet salt."

What do we mean by, "The proof is in the pudding"?

"The proof is in the pudding" means that the outcome is uncertain until the task is completed. The expression began as, "The proof of the pudding is in the eating." Pudding wasn't always exclusively a dessert. When the expression was coined, a pudding was any food presented in a solid mass and was often a main course, such as Yorkshire pudding. Popularized in 1605 by Cervantes in *Don Quixote* the saying has been traced back to 1300. Today, "the proof is in the pudding" means that you can't tell the value of something simply by its appearance.

What's the origin of ketchup?

In the 1690s the Chinese mixed together a tasty concoction of pickled fish and spices and called it *ke-tsiap*. By the early 1700s, the table sauce had made it to Malaysia, where it was discovered by British explorers, and by 1740, it had become an English staple. Fifty years later, North Americans added tomatoes to the Chinese recipe, and ketchup as we now know it had arrived. Tomatoes were considered poisonous for most of the eighteenth century because they're a close relative to the toxic belladonna and nightshade plants.

Why is an altered alcoholic drink called a "mickey"?

A mickey is an alcoholic drink that's been altered to incapacitate the person who drinks it. It's become a very dangerous idea, especially for young women, but it started out innocently enough in a Chicago bar owned by a man named Mickey Finn. Around the turn of the twentieth century, Finn discovered that he could get rid of an obnoxious customer by slipping a diarrheic into his drink. Within minutes the troublesome drinker would have urgently left the bar.

If it wasn't the French, then who invented french fries?

The Belgians are crazy about french fries; as a matter of fact, fries are their national dish, and they've been eating them with buckets of mussels since the mid-1800s. The French also claim inventing fries, because to "french" any food means to cut it very thin. The problem is that the Belgian claim predates the French technique by about fifty years. Usually this discussion ignores the fact that 40 percent of Belgians speak French, so they can take the credit.

The largest producer of french fries in the world is McCain Foods Limited, a Canadian company in Florenceville, New Brunswick. McCain has thirty potato processing plants on six continents around the world.

Why do we call that delicious crustacean a "lobster"?

The average lobster weighs about two pounds, and even though Shediac, New Brunswick, promotes itself as the Lobster Capital of the World, the largest lobster caught was in Nova Scotia and weighed 44.4 pounds. Before the twentieth century, eating lobster was a mark of poverty because to many people they resemble an insect, which is why their Latin name is *locusta*, meaning "locust," which led to the name "lobster."

Which restaurant meals do North Americans like best?

North Americans eat about half of their meals away from home. 55 percent of the average diet is fast food or junk food, but at a sit-down restaurant, fried chicken is the most popular meal, followed by roast beef, spaghetti, turkey, ham, and fried shrimp. On the other hand, Kentucky Fried Chicken sells approximately eleven pieces of chicken annually for every man, woman, and child in both Canada and the United States.

How did the eggplant get that name?

An eggplant is actually a fruit, but it is eaten like a vegetable. Originally from Southeast Asia, the eggplant was taken to Africa by the Persians.

In the eighth century AD, the eggplant was introduced to Europe through Spain by the Arabs. It was given its name by Europeans in the middle of the eighteenth century because the plant they knew had white or yellowish fruit the same shape and size as goose eggs.

How did marmalade get its name?

Legend has it that whenever the French-speaking Mary, Queen of Scots, wasn't feeling well, she would insist on a medicinal concoction made with boiled oranges. The orders the kitchen received were that Marie was *malade*, which is French for "sick," leading to "Marie malade," or marmalade. This, of course, is untrue. *Marmalade* is from the Portuguese word for the orange jam, which is *marmelada*, and it was popular long before the Scottish queen was born.

ANIMALS

Why does shedding crocodile tears mean that you're faking sadness?

Crocodiles have a nasty habit of sounding like a baby crying, which can attract naive human prey. While lying motionless in the sun, often hidden by tall grass, a crocodile waiting for lunch might leave its mouth open, which puts pressure on its tear glands, causing the illusion of crying. Like their phony human counterparts, they shed tears without any sense of contrition or sadness.

How did an American bird get named after the distant country of Turkey?

In 1519, conquistador Hernando Cortez returned to Spain with a bird introduced to him by the Native Americans of Mexico. The peculiar bird confused all of Europe. The French thought it was from India and so named it *dindon* (from *pouletes d'Inde*). Although the Germans, Dutch, and Swedes agreed that the bird was Indian they named it *kilcon* after Calcutta. By the time the trend reached England, rumour had it that the bird was from Turkey, and so that became its name.

How are things going if you're living "high on the hog"?

Living high on the hog meant originally that you ate what were regarded as the superior cuts of meat, the ones on the higher parts of the animal — pork chops, hams, etc. — as against the belly, feet, knuckles, jowls, and the like. Someone who lives high on the hog is therefore, in the extended sense, pretty well off.

Why is someone worn out "at the end of his rope"?

This expression evolved from the phrase "at the end of his tether." Such a phrase would have been used to describe a dog or a horse being tied or tethered. The old phrase was meant to convey a sense of self-restraint, while the new suggests that one has reached or exceeded one's defined boundaries.

Is there a difference in the quality between brown and white chicken eggs?

Chickens need between twenty-four and twenty-six hours to produce one egg. After a half-hour rest, they start the process over again. Occasionally they will stop laying and rest from between three to ten days. The colour of the eggs' shells has nothing to do with their quality. Brown eggs come from hens with red feathers and red earlobes, while white eggs come from chickens with white feathers and white earlobes.

What do chickens have to do with chicken pox?

Chickens have nothing to do with chicken pox. It was so named to distinguish the weaker form of the highly contagious but usually nonfatal

pox from the dreaded and extremely deadly form of smallpox. Because smallpox was named first, doctors needed a timid name for its less lethal cousin. To make it clear, they chose the unscientific but unassuming *chicken*.

Where did we get the saying "Not enough room to swing a cat"?

This colourful phrase evokes strange images of feline cruelty. In fact, it has nothing to do with cats, but the real story is at least as cruel. The "cat" is a cat-o'-nine-tails, a type of whip used to discipline sailors on old sailing ships. The cat-o'-nine-tails has one handle attached to nine thin strips of leather, each perhaps three feet long. The cat-o'-nine-tails would be used to administer lashings that would sting and leave welts on the recipient. The whippings would take place on the deck, because below deck there was not enough ceiling height to swing a cat (o'-nine-tails).

Why does March come "in like a lion and out like a lamb"?

When March weather roars "in like a lion," the adage suggests that the end of the month will leave like a lamb. This is because during early March, the constellation Leo is rising in the east, crossing the meridian on March 20. Therefore, the lion is associated with spring. At the same time the constellation Aries the ram (or the lamb) is setting in the west. So every March is "in like a lion and out like a lamb."

Why is a leader of a trend called a "bellwether"?

The metaphorical use of *bellwether* to mean a human leader dates back to the fifteenth century; its modern use usually means a company that sets an industry standard. A *wether* is in fact a castrated ram or male sheep, and a *bellwether* is the leader of the flock. He knows the routine, and he wears a bell so that the shepherd knows where his sheep are, because all the others will follow the bellwether anywhere without hesitation.

Why are Dalmatians used as mascots by firefighters?

Ancient Egyptian hieroglyphs show Dalmatians running with chariots. In Britain, they were used to escort carriages over hundreds of miles before standing guard while travellers stopped to eat or rest. Throughout the centuries the breed developed an affinity with horses, which is why they were a natural for early firefighters. The Dalmatians ran with the fire wagon and then kept the horses in line while the firefighters fought the blaze.

Dalmatians are from Dalmatia in a region of what is now Croatia. They were spread across Europe by the Roma people. Endurance, strength, and loyalty are their greatest characteristics.

Why do geese fly in a V formation?

When geese fly in either a V formation or a single line, they are drafting off the one in front in the same way that racecar drivers use each other to pick up speed. The lead or dominant bird, which is always a female, begins a turbulence wave that helps lift the birds behind her. The farther back in the flock, the less energy they need to fly. The lead bird rotates position to fight exhaustion.

The Wright brothers were inspired by the same principle of flight!

What part did Newfoundland play in naming the penguin?

The now extinct great auk of the North Atlantic was a large bird with small wings, making it very similar in appearance to the Antarctic penguin that we know today. Because of these underdeveloped wings, the auk was called a "pin-wing," and so in 1578, when the first description of the bird came out of Newfoundland, it was written as it sounded in the local dialect. *Pin-wing* became *penguin*. The name and the spelling were then given to the auk's southern look-alike. Coincidentally, the auk's Latin name is *pinguinis*.

Why are long, rambling, and unfunny stories called "shaggy dog stories"?

A shaggy dog story usually takes forever to tell and has a clever (if not funny) ending. The joy is found within the skill and craft of the narrator. During the 1930s and '40s a series of such jokes involving shaggy dogs circulated as a fad. A collection of these stories was published in 1946. Today, any rambling story ending in a pun is called a "shaggy dog story."

Here's one of the original shaggy dog stories: A grand householder in Park Lane, London, lost his very valuable and rather shaggy dog. The owner advertised repeatedly in the *Times*, but without luck, and finally he gave up hope. When an American in New York saw the advertisement, he was moved by the man's devotion and took great trouble to seek out another dog that matched the one in the advertisement. He found a perfect match. During his next business trip to London, he sought out the grieving owner's impressive house, where he was received in the householder's absence by a very English butler, who glanced at the dog, bowed, and exclaimed, in a horror-stricken voice, "But not so shaggy as that, sir!"

If you're wrong, why do we say you're "barking up the wrong tree"?

"Barking up the wrong tree" comes from hunting raccoons. Hunters use dogs to track down the little masked bandits, who will run into underbrush and, if cornered, climb a tree. When the dogs find that tree, they park under it barking and baying until the brave human arrives with the gun, only to often find that the raccoon has outsmarted the dogs by crossing the branches to another tree and freedom.

When we want a dog to attack, why do we say, "Sic 'em"?

Dogs are descended from wolves and interact with humans the same as they would with other dogs within a pack. They are protective of their family or pack and instinctively attack only when hunting or frightened. This behaviour can be altered in some dogs through aggressive training. Guard dogs have to learn to attack on command from the human alpha dog, their trainer. "Sic 'em," a very old command, is an abbreviation of "seek him."

Why do we say that a new subject is "a horse of a different colour"?

"A horse of a different colour" is a separate issue from the business at hand and comes from horse trading. When horses are born, their official registration includes a record of their colour. To make sure they were buying the horse pedigree as advertised, traders learned to check this registration to ensure that the colt's colour was the same as the one for sale, otherwise they were being cheated with a "horse of a different colour."

Why is the height of a horse measured in hands?

For five thousand years, the height of a horse has been measured in hands. Body parts were our first points of reference for measurement. For example, a foot was exactly that: the length of a Roman foot. A hand was measured with the thumb curled into the palm, a distance now standardized as four inches. A horse's height is measured in a straight line from the ground to the withers (the top of the shoulders between the neck and the back).

A horse of 15.2 hands measures 15 times 4 inches, plus 2 inches, or 62 inches. It's important to keep in mind that you can have 15.3 hands, but after the next full inch the height is taken as 16 hands, not 15.4.

The hand is a tradition of British measurement. In the rest of Europe a horse's height is measured in metres and centimetres. In some places, like Europe and South Africa, they measure in both hands and centimetres.

HOLIDAYS

What is the religious significance of Groundhog Day?

February 2 is an ancient Christian holiday celebrating Mary's purification and is known as Candlemas Day. Christians believed that if the day dawned sunny, crop planting would have to wait because winter would last six more weeks. During the 1880s, a few friends in Punxsutawney, Pennsylvania, went groundhog hunting every Candlemas Day. They became known as the Punxsutawney Groundhog Club, with a mascot named Phil.

Who receives the most Valentine's cards?

Valentine's Day is second only to Christmas as the largest annual card-sending holiday. One billion cards are sent each year! Women purchase 85 percent of all Valentine's cards, so men receive more, but then 15 percent of women send *themselves* flowers on February 14. In order of popularity, the cards are sent to teachers, children, mothers, wives, and sweethearts. As well, 3 percent of all Valentine's cards are sent to pets.

What are the origins of Ash Wednesday?

At the beginning of Lent, which always falls on a Wednesday, Catholics mark their foreheads with a cross made of ashes to symbolize their commitment to Christ. The ashes are from burned palm fronds used in the previous year's celebration of Palm Sunday. In ancient times, when someone died, it was a mourning custom to sit inside and cover one's head and body with dust and ashes as a mortal reminder that we are all "from ashes to ashes and dust to dust."

Why is the season of Easter fasting called "Lent"?

Lent begins on Ash Wednesday and is the forty-day fast that precedes Easter. The forty days are an imitation of Christ's preparation for his ministry, which reached its climax with the crucifixion and resurrection. The word *Lent* has no religious significance whatsoever. It comes from the Old English word *Lencten*, which was the Anglo-Saxon name for the season we now call spring, within which Easter is celebrated.

In all languages other than English, the season of Easter fasting has a name derived from the Latin term *Quadragesima*, or "the forty days."

How did the white trumpet lily become the Easter lily?

During the 1880s, while in Bermuda, Mrs. Thomas Sargent became enamoured with the beautiful white Bermuda trumpet lily. She took its bulbs back to Philadelphia, where it caught on among local florists. Since it blooms in spring, the flower soon became known as the "Easter lily," and its popularity spread. The lily had been introduced to Bermuda from its native Japan and is now grown primarily on North America's Pacific coast.

Why do Orthodox and Catholic churches celebrate holy days on different dates?

By the mid-sixteenth century the Julian calendar was out of whack with the lunar calendar by eleven full days. In 1582, Pope Gregory XIII made an eleven-day adjustment so that October 4 was followed by October 15. A system of leap years was designed to keep the calendar in line. Catholics adopted the Gregorian calendar, while the Orthodox Church continued using the ancient Julian calendar for celebrations of Christmas and Easter.

Eastern Orthodox churches continue to use the Julian calendar today. It is currently thirteen days later than the Gregorian calendar.

Since 1923, the Romanian Orthodox and Greek Orthodox churches have adopted the Gregorian calendar. However, they continue to use the Julian calendar for Easter calculations.

The gap between the two calendars continues to grow. Most Greek Orthodox churches currently celebrate Christmas on January 7 and New Year's Day on January 14 (according to the Gregorian calendar). This gap generally places Easter celebrations on the same Sunday in the Roman Catholic and Eastern Orthodox churches only once every three to four years. During non-leap years, Orthodox Easter is delayed by one, four, or five weeks.

Why do Canadians celebrate Victoria Day?

To most Canadians, May 24 signals the start of gardening season, but it's also a memory of what was once called Empire Day, when the people living on 20 percent of the Earth's land surface owed allegiance to the British Crown. For sixty-four of its three hundred years, the Empire was presided over by Queen Victoria. Canada has celebrated Victoria Day on May 24 since 1845. Nowadays, the May 24 holiday celebrates the birthday of the current monarch.

Why do we refer to the celebrants of the first Thanksgiving as "Pilgrims"?

The New World settlers from the *Mayflower* weren't called Pilgrims until two hundred years after their 1620 arrival at Plymouth Rock. It was Daniel Webster, in a bicentennial celebration of their landing, who first described them as "Our Pilgrim Fathers." The word comes from a Latin derivative meaning a traveller. *Perager* became *pelegrin*, then *pilegrim* in English, evolving into *pilgrim*. "Pilgrim" was first used to describe Christians who made a journey of religious devotion to the Holy Land.

How did bobbing for apples become a Halloween tradition?

Halloween was the Celts' most significant annual holiday. After the Romans invaded Britain, they respected and adopted a few of the Celtic practices, and during the first century AD, the two cultures began integrating their late autumn rituals. In October, the Romans celebrated Pomona, the goddess of fruit and trees. Her symbol was an apple, which is how that fruit, whether bobbing for it or otherwise, became symbolic of Halloween.

Why do children ask us to shell out treats on Halloween?

As a challenge to Halloween, the Roman Catholic Church placed All Saints Day on November 1. On that day, Christians went from village to village begging for soul cakes, a mixture of bread and currants. One cake bought one prayer for the souls of the donor's departed relatives. The phrase "shell out" as a demand for payment comes from the shelling of dried peas or corn, once a currency of commercial exchange among the poor.

How did the poinsettia, a Mexican weed, become associated with Christmas?

One hundred years ago, Dr. Joel Poinsett, the American ambassador to Mexico, introduced the plant to the rest of North America. A Mexican legend has it that two poor children had nothing to offer the baby Jesus during the Christmas festival, so on their way to church they picked some green weeds from the road side. When they placed them at the nativity the green petals turned a bright red in the shape of a star.

Is *Xmas* a disrespectful commercial abbreviation of *Christmas*?

Xmas has its roots legitimately grounded in the Greek word for Christ, which is *Xristos*. In the sixteenth century, Europeans adopted the first letter from Xristos as an initial for Christ's name, and even though the practice had been common among the early Christians, some North Americans, not understanding the Greek language, mistakenly took the X as a commercial insult.

When exactly are the twelve days of Christmas?

The twelve days of Christmas are the days separating December 25 and the Epiphany, or the date of Christ's baptism, which is January 6 — the legendary date that the three Wise Men visited the stable with their gifts. It was once the custom to pile up gifts on December 25 and then distribute them over the days leading to January 6. In North America, the tradition is now only a memory through the carol "The Twelve Days of Christmas."

How did Christmas cake become a tradition?

A dish of porridge that once ended the fast on Christmas Eve evolved into a pudding with dried fruits and spices as a tribute to the Wise Men. By the sixteenth century, the pudding had become a fruitcake, served during the parish priest's home blessings on Twelfth Night. In 1870, after the protestant Queen Victoria banned Twelfth Night celebrations because they were "unchristian," clever confectioners began selling their fruitcakes as "Christmas cake."

Why are fruits and nuts offered over Christmas?

December 21 is the day of the winter solstice: the year's shortest day and longest night. It's known as St. Thomas Day, commemorating the last apostle to be convinced of Christ's resurrection. On this day a bowl of nuts and fruits is put on display to ensure prosperity in the new year, and by sharing these, the wish is extended to friends and neighbours. Failure to share this providence could mean a lean crop in the following seasons.

Why do we hang stockings at Christmas?

According to legend, the very first gifts St. Nicholas gave were to three very poor girls who needed money for their wedding dowries. On Christmas Eve they hung their stockings to dry by the fireplace. St. Nicholas slipped in at night and left gold coins in each of their stockings so they could marry the men they loved. Until recently, Christmas stockings were filled with nuts and fruit. The Italians introduced giving a lump of coal to naughty children.

What's the story behind "O Little Town of Bethlehem"?

In 1865, inspired by a horseback trip from Jerusalem to Bethlehem, Reverend Philip Brooks of Philadelphia composed a poem, which he eventually showed to Lewis Redner, the organist at the Church of the Holy Trinity, wondering if he could put the words to music. Redner was stumped — that is, until Christmas Eve, when it came to him in a dream. The next morning, the carol we know as "O Little Town of Bethlehem" was born.

What's the story behind "Silent Night"?

On Christmas Eve in 1817, when Father Joseph Mohr of St. Nicholas Church in Arnsdorf, Austria, found that a mouse had chewed through the bellows of his church pipe organ, he rushed to the home of music teacher Franz Gruber. The two men quickly wrote a musical piece, hoping it would save the Christmas Mass. With Father Mohr playing guitar, they sang their song in harmony to a small Austrian congregation who became the first to hear the most beloved carol of them all — "Silent Night."

"Silent Night" was performed by troupes of Tyrolean Folk Singers, but by 1848, when Father Mohr died penniless at fifty-five, "Silent Night" had fallen into obscurity. In 1854, King Frederick William IV of Prussia heard the song and was so moved, he became responsible for its revival.

Why is Christmas referred to as "the Yuletide"?

The ancient Germanic peoples celebrated the winter solstice with a feast day for the pagan sun god Jul, which is still the preferred Scandinavian reference to Christmas and survives in our Yule log. Fearing the sun god had disappeared during the year's longest night, a vigil was held from dusk to dawn and the Yule log was lit to encourage the sun's return and to discourage evil spirits returning to the Earth's surface.

It was Pope Gregory I who suggested that missionaries not challenge the northern pagan practices and traditions, but rather transfer their meaning to Christianity.

The Yuletide covers all December feast days, including Chanukah.

How was the date of Christmas established?

Early scholars believed that prophets died on an anniversary of their birth. Once they established Good Friday as either March 25 or April 6, they reasoned that Christ's incarnation was nine months later, which would be either December 25 or January 6. The choice was not simply to comply with pagan superstitions; in 386 AD, when the date was established, any date would have collided with pagan rituals because they filled the calendar year.

Neither the date of Christ's birthday nor that of his crucifixion is given in the Gospels.

Why do we light the Christmas tree?

In the sixteenth century, Germans began decorating fir trees with ribbons, flowers, apples, and coloured paper. Inspired by the reflection of stars off branches in the forest, Martin Luther placed lit candles on his indoor tree. After three hundred years of candles, Edward Johnson introduced electric Christmas lights outside his Fifth Avenue home in New York in 1882. Johnson also worked on the invention of the light bulb with Thomas Edison.

Which Jewish tradition still influences Christmas celebrations?

The celebration of Christmas begins with Midnight Mass, and the calendar date is December 25, but every Christian knows that the reverence begins on Christmas Eve. Christmas Eve comes directly from the Jewish custom of beginning religious rituals with ceremonies starting at sundown the evening before the holy day with candles and prayers lasting until the following sundown — in this case, Christmas Day.

Considering his workload, how much time does Santa spend at each child's home?

Travelling at about a thousand miles a second, or 3.6 million miles an hour, Santa covers 111 million miles in 31 hours. Within one second he must visit 500,000 homes, which is why we seldom see him. Of course he does have help, and in some cases he delivers presents before Christmas or even works on Boxing Day, but it's still very hard work.

When is the proper time to take down the Christmas tree?

From the very beginning of Christmas traditions, January 6 — the day of the Epiphany — was the official end of gift giving, and the most popular day of the celebration. Some people still celebrate the Epiphany as being more important than Christmas Day. Regardless, January 6 is the last day of the festival, and that is the day to take down the tree and decorations. To do otherwise is bad luck.

What's the story behind Chanukah?

The word *Chanukah* means "rededication." Over 2,300 years ago, the Syrians occupying Judea were overthrown by a Jewish army led by Judah Maccabee. The Syrians had desecrated the Jerusalem Temple with their own gods; while cleaning and reclaiming the temple, the Israelites found enough oil to light the eternal lamp for only one day, but incredibly the flame flickered for eight days, a miracle celebrated to this day as the "Festival of Lights."

The Syrians, led by King Antiochus, had ordered the Jewish people to reject their God and customs and replace them with Greek symbols and deities.

The rededication of the temple was on the twenty-fifth day of the ancient month of Kislev (scholars are uncertain whether this was in the new calendar months of November or December).

The Jewish army fought for years, led by Judah Maccabee and his four brothers.

Maccabee means "hammer."

Judea was in, part, what is now Israel.

What's the story behind Kwanza?

Kwanza is a seven-day celebration beginning the day after Christmas. It was created in 1966 by Maulana Karenga, chairman of African studies at California State University, and is based on an African winter harvest. *Kwanza* means "first fruits" in Swahili and celebrates African heritage. On each night of Kwanza, one of several candles is lit and gifts reflecting creativity and community are exchanged.

Kwanza is based on seven principles: *umoja* means unity, *kujichag-ulla* means self-determination, *ujima* means collective work and responsibility, *ujamaa* means cooperative economics, *nia* means purpose, *kuumba* means creativity, and *imani* means faith.

Why do the Chinese name each year for an animal?

The Chinese have tied animal names to calendar years for centuries. According to the myth, Buddha invited all the animals on Earth to visit him on New Year's Day, but only twelve arrived. They were the rat, the ox, the tiger, the hare, the dragon, the snake, the horse, the sheep, the monkey, the rooster, the dog, and the pig. As a reward, Buddha honoured each of these twelve with a year of its own.

Why is New Year's Eve celebrated with noisemakers and kissing strangers?

New Year's Eve is the night of Holy Sylvester, the Pope who converted the Roman Emperor Constantine to Christianity. With the Emperor's conversion, pagan gods fell from favour but fought back through the souls of the living. To combat their return, during the darkness of New Year's Eve, people wandered the streets shouting to strangers, frolicking with noisemakers, and generally acting foolish — a custom that resurfaces every New Year's Eve.

Pope Sylvester I (314–335 AD) cured the Emperor Constantine of leprosy.

Some New Year's Eve revellers disguised themselves as mummers so that the demoted gods couldn't identify and punish them as they wandered the streets.

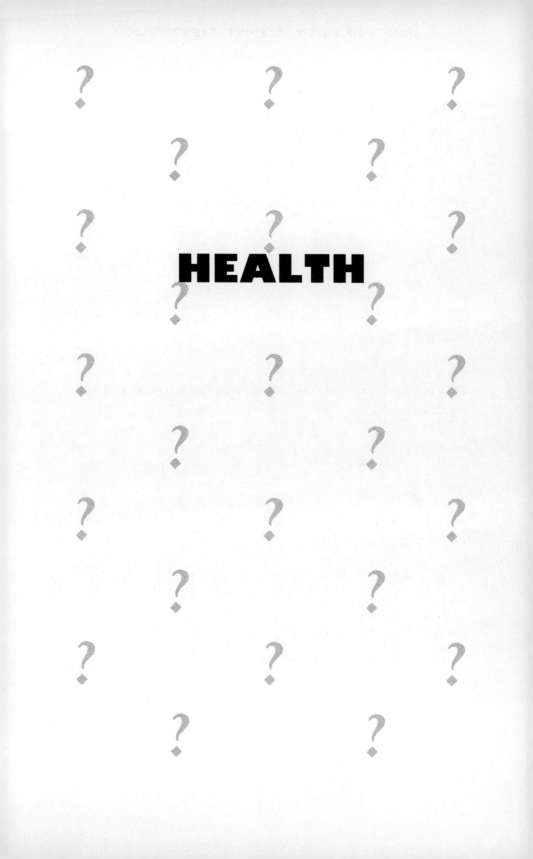

HEALTH

Why do doctors on television use the word *stat* in an emergency?

It was the Romans who gave the practice of medicine its prestige, and consequently, other than the church, no other profession is still as influenced by Latin. When a doctor says, "Stat!" he is abbreviating *statim*, meaning "immediately." The use of the word stands out from "Quickly!" or "Hurry!" and conveys urgency; and yes, it's still used by real doctors outside of television.

Why do we say we are "under the weather" when we get sick?

When the weather turned bad at sea, the constant rolling of the rough water caused a rocking motion that brought on seasickness. Those passengers affected were taken below deck, because the sway diminishes the lower you get on the ship (especially down near the keel). Those taken below deck because of seasickness were brought "under the weather."

Why is the word *quarantine* used to describe enforced isolation of contagious diseases?

Before the age of modern epidemiology, attempts to control the outbreak of a contagious disease included an arbitrary forty days of enforced confinement. New and strange diseases were often carried from abroad by ships, so a quarantine of crew and cargo helped discourage epidemics. Forty days was chosen because of its prominence in the Bible. *Quarante* is the French for forty, and *quarantine* literally translates to "forty-ish."

Why, after a routine medical checkup, do we say we've received a "clean bill of health"?

If you say a doctor has given you a clean bill of health, you're using a nautical expression from the days when sailing ships were required to obtain a document from local officials at every port of call declaring that they had not been exposed to any epidemic or infectious disease.

If they didn't have this bill of health, the next port would quarantine the ship, crew, and cargo for forty days.

Why is a terrible or fake doctor called a "quack"?

The first reference to a healer as a quack goes back into the sixteenth century, when it was common for dubious medicine men to travel from

town to town dispensing their miracle cures from the back of a horse-drawn wagon. The quack refers to the meaningless sound of a duck, which had the same validity as the claims made by the medicine men that their salves or ointments had healing powers. Today's quacks still dispense bad medicine.

Why is reconstructive surgery called "plastic"?

Plastic surgery was first practiced in India around 600 BC when noses that had been amputated as punishment for criminals were reconstructed with skin from the forehead. The word *plastic* is from the ancient Greek word *plastikos*, which means "to mold into shape." The plastic arts include sculpting and ceramics. The modern term "plastic surgery" came from a surgical handbook published in 1838.

The word *plastique* for reconstructive surgery was introduced in 1798 by a French surgeon named Desault.

Why do we get sweaty palms when we're nervous?

If your palms sweat when you're nervous, you can blame evolution. The inside of your hands have more sweat glands than any other part of your body. This is because tens of thousands of years ago, when our primal ancestors were threatened by savage carnivores, the quickest exit was the nearest tree. Stress caused their palms to sweat, and the moisture gave them a better grip on the branches and vines they were climbing.

What is the history of Aspirin?

Aspirin is the most successful pharmaceutical drug ever produced. Its main ingredient is found in the bark of the willow tree and was known as a pain reliever in 1500 B.C. In 1828, the ingredient salicin was isolated. In 1897 chemist Felix Hoffman developed a synthetic form, known as acetylsalicylic acid, at the Bayer factory in Germany; it was referred to as "Aspirin" for the first time in 1899.

The word *salicin*, the compound in the willow bark that relieves pain, is derived from *salix*, the Latin word for "willow tree." North American Indians used birch bark to make salicylate pain remedies.

137 million Aspirin tablets are taken every day. In 1915, Aspirin became available without prescription.

Bayer® produces 50,000 tons of acetylsalicylic acid each year — enough to produce 100 billion tablets. If these tablets were laid side by side they would form a line stretching to the moon and back.

AMERICANS & CANADIANS

What do the images on the American flag represent?

The American flag has changed twenty-six times since the first official design was approved by the Continental Congress on June 14, 1777. Today it consists of thirteen horizontal stripes, seven red alternating with six white. The stripes represent the original thirteen colonies, while the stars represent the fifty states of the Union. The colors of the flag are symbolic as well: red represents hardiness and valour, white represents purity and innocence, and blue represents vigilance, perseverance, and justice.

How did the American flag come to be known as "Old Glory"?

This famous name was coined by Captain William Driver, a shipmaster of Salem, Massachusetts, in 1831. As he was leaving on one of his many voyages aboard the brig *Charles Doggett* — one that would climax with the rescue of the mutineers of the *Bounty* — some friends presented him with a beautiful flag of twenty-four stars. As the banner opened to the ocean breeze for the first time, he exclaimed, "Old Glory!"

How many former American presidents are not buried in the United States?

As of 2005, there are five former American presidents not buried in the United States. Ulysses S. Grant is not buried but is entombed in New York (a body is only buried when it's placed in the ground and covered with dirt). The others are Presidents Gerald Ford, Jimmy Carter, Bill Clinton, and the current president's father, George Herbert Walker Bush, who are all still alive.

Why does "Hail to the Chief" introduce the American president?

When the American President enters a room, "Hail to the Chief "is preceded by a fanfare of four drum and bugle ruffles and flourishes.

The number of ruffles and flourishes indicates the importance of the person being introduced — not "Hail to the Chief," which is from the English dramatization of Sir Walter Scott's poem "The Lady of the Lake" and which became a popular band number for introducing any important person around 1812.

As a fanfare, four ruffles and flourishes is the highest American honour.

President Carter did away with "Hail to the Chief" for a time during his term.

Because it was a popular melody commonly used for dignitaries, there is no record of when "Hail to the Chief" made the transition into a signature for the president. It just evolved.

In 1810, James Sanderson wrote to a friend that Scott's "The Lady of the Lake" was being made into a play in London. Soon after, Scott received a note from an army officer friend including the music for the Boat Song, now known as "Hail to the Chief."

Why was George M. Cohan forced to rewrite "It's A Grand Old Flag"?

In 1906, George M. Cohan was forced to change one word in his anthem to the American flag, which begins, "It's a grand old flag/it's a high flying flag..." Though today it's sung as a tribute to Old Glory, if Cohan hadn't made the change, the song probably would never be sung. Cohan's original lyrics started with, "It's a grand old *rag* ..."

Why are Americans called "Yankees"?

It's said that *Yankee* comes from an English pirate reference to the Dutch, who were known for their diet of cheese, which in their own language is Kaas. The Christian name *Jan* tied to the word *Kaas*, or Jan-Kaas (pronounced "yan-kas"), was a derogatory English reference to the Dutch who settled New York. However, it's more likely that *Yankees* evolved from *yengees*, an early Native American pronunciation of *Anglais*, the French word for the English who had settled the northeast.

Why do Americans call Canadians "Canucks"?

The word *canuck* first appeared in 1835 as a derogatory American reference to French Canadians working in the lumber camps of Maine. Today it means any Canadian and is no longer an insult unless used by non-Canadians to describe our French brothers. It's most likely a combination of the French word for canoeman, *canaque*, with the "uk" exaggerated from a very common ending to Indian nouns like Tuktoyuktuk.

But the word could also be from Canada/Kanata (the name derived from a First Nations word meaning "a collection of huts"), abbreviated with "uk" as a suffix.

Over a million French Canadians migrated to New England during the second half of the nineteenth century. Jack Kerouac's family was among them.

Johnny Canuck, the cartoon character, dates from 1869 and was used for propaganda during the Second World War.

Is it proper to call Canada's northern Natives *Eskimo* or *Inuit*?

Legend has it that the word *Eskimo* was picked up from the Abenaki by European explorers as meaning "eaters of raw meat," but the word was originally *ayashkinew* and referred to the way they tied their snowshoes. It is not a derogatory word, although erroneously believing this and responding to demands from Eskimo political associations, Canada replaced *Eskimo* with *Inuit*, meaning "human being," in the 1970s. Outside of Canada, Arctic Natives are still called Eskimo.

The Eskimo are the native inhabitants of the seacoasts of the Arctic and sub-Arctic regions of North America and the northeastern tip of Siberia. Their habitation area extends over four countries.

The term *Eskimo* is still used in Alaska, whether or not they are Eskimos culturally or linguistically. For example, while the Yupik people prefer to be called Yup'ik, they do not generally object to being called Eskimo, but they do not consider themselves Inuit.

The Inuit Circumpolar Conference meeting in Barrow, Alaska, in 1977 officially adopted Inuit as a designation for all Eskimo peoples, regardless of their local usages.

HISTORY

Why do most spiral staircases ascend in a clockwise direction?

Spiral staircases originated as a defence mechanism in medieval castles because all knights were right-handed. Southpaws were considered under the Devil's influence and were automatically disqualified for knighthood. While ascending a clockwise spiral staircase backwards with a sword in his right hand, the defending knight could freely swing his sword arm, while the attacker was neutralized by the wall blocking his own right arm.

Why is the night shift called "the graveyard shift"?

During the Victorian era — before embalming — there was a great fear of being buried alive. Wealthy men and women arranged to have a string tied to their hands that ran from the buried coffin to a bell on the surface, so that if they awoke they could sound the alarm. The cemetery was busy during the day, but someone was needed to wander the grounds and listen for the bells during the night. This was called the graveyard shift.

Why do American broadcasting stations use the call letters *K* and *W*?

During the 1920s, while radio was in its infancy, the FCC assigned the letter *K* to all stations west of the Mississippi and the letter *W* to all those east of the river. Exceptions were made for stations with established call signs, like KDKA in Pittsburgh, and those affiliated with a network. The other three letters are the broadcaster's choice.

Why is a dicey situation considered a "hazard"?

A potentially dangerous situation was first called a hazard by the western European Crusaders after returning from the Holy Land, where they encountered and were fleeced by unscrupulous local gamblers using loaded or doctored dice. "Hazard" is how they pronounced *al zahr*, which is the Arabic word for dice. In time *hazardous*, like *dicey*, became a reference to anything associated with risk.

What does the "post" mean in "post office," and what is the "mail"?

In medieval Europe, a system of roads was built to speed messages from the heads of state to all corners of the realm. These were called post roads because riders on horseback were "posted" at intervals in a relay system copied by the Pony Express to speed the delivery of the mail. *Mail* is what they called the pouch that carried the letters. Urgent messages were marked "post-haste."

Did St. Patrick rid Ireland of snakes? And what is a leprechaun's profession?

There were never any snakes in Ireland. The story of St. Patrick banishing snakes from Ireland is a metaphor for the eradication of paganism during the fifth century. St. Patrick did, however, superimpose a circle representing the sun, a powerful pagan symbol, on what is known as the Celtic cross. As for leprechauns, these two-foot-tall creatures are employed as shoemakers for other fairies.

What medieval profession would you have if you heard the "highly strung Mr. Stringer tell Mr. Archer point-blank to brace himself for a quarrel"?

If you heard Stringer tell Archer point-blank to brace himself for a quarrel, you were probably an archer. Surnames taken from archery include Stringer, Bower, Fletcher, Abbott (meaning, "at the butts"), and of course Archer. Point-blank is the bulls-eye on a French target. "Brace yourself" meant prepare to shoot, while a quarrel is an arrow shot from a crossbow.

Archery was taken so seriously that Henry I of England passed a law that dismissed any punishment for anyone who killed someone while practising.

Where did our last names come from?

In the Middle Ages, most common people didn't have a last name. Many of our familiar surnames came from the necessity to distinguish between two people with the same first name by adding their occupation, location, or a physical characteristic. William the tanner and William the blacksmith became William Tanner and William Smith. Poor country people who worked the land took the name of their land lord, so a regal surname usually doesn't mean regal ancestry.

Other occupational last names:

Taylor — makes or repairs clothing
Carter — makes or repairs carts
Miller — ground flour from grain
Wainwright — wagon builder
Bishop — worked with a bishop

Last names with geographic origins:

Atwood — one who lives near the forest
Eastman — one who is from east of here
Westwood — one who is from the western forest
Dunlop — from the muddy hill
Churchill — lives near a church on a hill

What is the origin of nicknames?

Nicknames are usually pet names of endearment or affection and are derived from a distinct characteristic of or the appearance of the subject. The source is the Old English word *eke*, which means "as well as" or "in addition to." The linguistic transition to *nick*, meaning "devilish," came later. To a stranger a nickname signalled the kind of person they were dealing with by exaggerating either the person's good or bad characteristics.

Does every family have a coat of arms?

There is no such thing as a family coat of arms. They were granted only to individuals, and those individuals were exclusively men. A coat of arms can only be used by the uninterrupted line of male descendants of the person to whom it was granted and is a privilege of nobility. The heraldic symbol was emblazoned on a warrior's shield and was also added to the fabric coat worn on the outside of his armor, which is why it's known as a coat of arms.

Heraldry is the language of symbols or emblems and is the lone surviving custom from the romance and barbarism of feudal times.

Blazoning is the heraldic term to describe a coat of arms.

The unique colour, shape, and design emblazoned on the warrior's shield all distinguished him as friend or foe on the battlefield.

Why do we refer to a single item of clothing as a "pair of pants"?

Pants is short for *pantaloons*, and the item only became a single garment late in its history. Up until the seventeenth century, the legs were covered with two separate sleeves of fabric called "hose," which were tied to a belt with braces. The open crotch was covered with breeches and a long tunic. The plural reference to a single unit as a "pair of pants" is extended to trousers, slacks, and shorts.

Pantaloons came from the comic wardrobe of a stock character in the Commedia dell'Arte.

Why do we say that someone snooping into our lives is "digging up the past"?

When someone is "looking for dirt," or scavenging for scandal in another's earlier life, if they dig long enough they're bound to find something. Of course if you're scrounging through an attic trunk or old scrapbooks, you too are "digging up the past." The expression logically comes from the science of archeology, where people make a profession of "digging up dirt" to understand the present by looking into the past.

Why are inappropriate actions called "taboo"?

If something is unacceptable, it's considered "taboo." When Captain James Cook visited the Friendly Islands in 1777, he noted in his diary that the Polynesians used the word *taboo* to signify that a thing was forbidden. Cook and his men carried the word to the rest of the English-speaking world, not realizing that it also means "go away," which is what the Islanders were telling him when he landed.

How do they calculate shoe sizes?

Roman shoemakers had discovered that the length of three barleycorns equaled one inch, so they used one kernel, or a third of an inch, as a measurement for shoe size. In 1324, King Edward of England decreed that three barleycorns was indeed one inch. In the seventeenth century, children's shoe sizes were deemed to be less than, and adult sizes more than, thirteen barleycorns. (Size zero was a baby's size, and the shoes went up in one-barleycorn increments to a children's thirteen, after which adult's sizes started again at one.) That calculation is still used to determine shoe sizes to this day.

Why is the telling of a tall tale said to be "spinning a yarn"?

If someone is "spinning a yarn" they are exaggerating the truth. First printed about 1812, the expression is nautical and has nothing to do with domestic spinning. Sailors were required to spend long tedious shifts working in pairs, spinning fibers into the endless miles of rope needed to keep their sailing ship sound. To pass the time, they entertained themselves by telling tall tales, or "spinning yarns."

POP CULTURE

Was cocaine ever an active ingredient in Coca-Cola?

When Coca-Cola was introduced in 1886 it was sold as a cure for sore throats, nervousness, headache, colds, neuralgia, and sleeplessness, and like other patent medicines of the time, its formula did include a secret amount of cocaine as well as an extract of cola leaves and kola nuts. As knowledge about the dangers of cocaine became known in the new century, the drug was reduced and eventually eliminated in 1929.

After spending $120 for supplies and advertising in their first year, Coca-Cola sold twenty-five bottles.

Coke® went public in 1919, and one share from that time is currently worth close to $100,000.

Who or what were the inspirations for naming the Baby Ruth chocolate bar, the Tootsie Roll, and Hershey's Kisses?

Confectioner Leo Hirschfield created the Tootsie Roll. He named his chewy chocolate treat after his daughter Clara, whose nickname was Tootsie. The Baby Ruth chocolate bar was named in honour of President Grover Cleveland's baby daughter, Ruth. Hershey's named their chocolate treats Kisses because in the factory the machine that dispenses them kisses the conveyor belt.

How did the bobby pin get its name?

The bobby pin got its name in the 1930s, but the inexpensive little wire gadget had become popular with flappers during the "Roaring 20s." A short haircut for young women came in vogue for the first time in history, and the bobby pin helped keep its shape. The *bob* in "bobby pins," like the one in "bobby socks," means "to cut short," and was previously used to describe the cropped or bobbed tail of a horse.

Who qualifies as a "metrosexual," and where did the term originate?

The word *metrosexual* was coined in 1994 by writer Mark Simpson. However, it was Simpson's 2002 article in *Salon* concerning soccer star David Beckham that introduced *metrosexual* to everyday use. A metrosexual is a straight but fastidious and style-conscious urban male whose self-indulgence never keeps him far from his true love — himself.

What does the title refer to in the book *The Lord of the Flies*?

When William Golding published his classic novel in 1954, he chose a title suggesting a powerful, malevolent, supernatural presence, which he called the Lord of the Flies. Translated into Hebrew, "Lord of the Flies" is *Ba'al zebhubh*, which, since the twelfth century in English has been rendered as "Beelzebub," a Catholic reference to the Devil. Therefore, the Lord of the Flies is the Devil.

Why, during a time of million-dollar prizes, do we still say, "That's the $64 question"?

In 1941, Bob Hawk emceed a radio quiz called *Take It or Leave It*. Chosen from a live studio audience, the contestants went through seven levels of difficulty, starting at $2 and culminating with a chance at $64. The show's success inspired a dozen imitators, but the original gave us the expression that stuck: "That's the $64 question."

What is the true inspiration for paranormal movies about men in black?

Since the start of the UFO phenomenon in 1947, many who experienced sightings have reported visits from men in black. After approaching Washington claiming that he had proof that flying saucers exist, Albert Bender was visited by three men dressed in black, after whose visit he became gravely ill and refused to elaborate. These men in black, who inspired the popular movies, have only been seen in America.

Why are coming attractions called "movie trailers"?

Movies used to be shown continuously without a break between features. If someone arrived late for a show they would simply sit and watch for where they came in before leaving. To catch this crowd, and to signify an end to the film as well as chase as many people as possible from their seats for a new audience, coming attractions were spliced onto the end of the first showing as a "trailer," even though it preceded the next screening.

Why did Sinatra and the rest of the Rat Pack call women "broads"?

In the eighteenth century, poker cards were called broads because they were wider than those used for other card games. Around 1912, because they resembled poker cards, tickets of admission, meal tickets, and transit tickets were being called "broads." By 1914, because they were a different kind of "meal ticket," pimps began calling their prostitutes "broads." Soon the term entered the underworld and was eventually picked up by entertainers.

Why are celebrity photographers called "paparazzi"?

The word *paparazzi* as a tag for pushy celebrity photographers comes from Frederico Fellini's 1960 film *La Dolce Vita* and first appeared in its current use around 1968. In the movie, the character Signor Paparazzo (the singular of paparazzi) was an obnoxious, creepy little man who was despised by the stars. Before Fellini used it, the word *papparazzo* was a word in an Italian dialect for "buzzing insect."

Why does *deadpan* mean an expressionless human face?

The word *deadpan* was first used in print by the *New York Times* in 1928 as a description of the great silent film comic Buster Keaton, who was also known as "The Great Stone Face." The theatrical slang use of *pan* for face dates to the fourteenth century. *Dead*, of course, means it's not moving, or it's expressionless.

Pancake makeup for an actor's pan was introduced in 1937 by Max Factor.

Why are the Sesame Street characters called Muppets?

The Muppets, who've had their own television show as well as a series of movies, are best known for their roles on *Sesame Street*, which first appeared in 1969. After 4,100 episodes, *Sesame Street* is the longest running television show in history and has received more Emmy Awards than any other show. The Muppets were Jim Henson's idea, and he named them by combing the words *marionette* and *puppet*.

What are the odds of winning on a Lotto 6/49 ticket?

The odds of winning on a Lotto 6/49 are 1 in 13,983,816, because that's how many different groups of six numbers can possibly be drawn. This means the odds of winning are about the same as flipping a coin and landing on heads twenty-four times in succession. The odds of winning second place are 1 in 2,330,635.

A recent Gallup Poll showed that 57 percent of North Americans have bought a lottery ticket in the last twelve months

The odds against hitting the jackpot on a slot machine are 889 to 1.

If you add together all the numbers on a roulette wheel (1 to 36), the total is the mystical number 666, often associated with the Devil.

Why is the mystical board game called a "Ouija board"?

The Ouija board has been around since the fourth century, but the first patent was obtained by a German professor of music in 1854. Parker Brothers purchased the rights in 1966 and published the Ouija board game in 1967. The game begins by asking if any spirits are present, and the desired answer is in the name: *Ouija* is a compound of *oui*, which is "yes" in French, and *ja*, which is "yes" in German, so Ouija means "yes, yes."

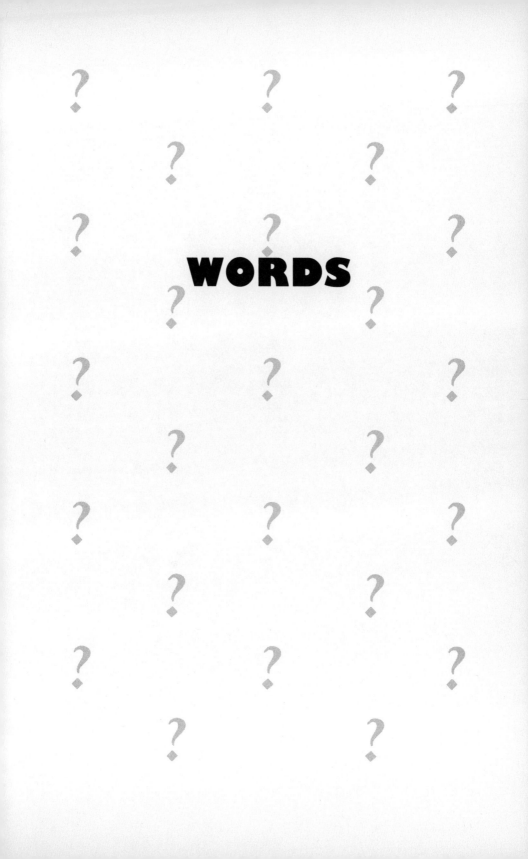

WORDS

Why is *spring* both a season and fresh water from the ground?

Spring is a season, but it's also part of a mattress, an underground water supply, and a surprise attack. Spring derives from *sprengh*, an ancient Indo-European word for "rapid movement." It was around 816 AD when *spring* was first used to mean "rising up," or the beginning of something. By the fourteenth century the first of the four seasons became the spring of the year.

Why is abduction for ransom called "kidnapping"?

The word *kidnap* was first recorded in 1666 and referred to the criminal practice of enticing children or apprentices to come away and be sold to sea captains who took them to British colonies to be sold as slaves, labourers, or indentured servants. *Kid* was an underworld reference to a child, while *nap*, a variation of *nab*, means to seize or steal. Today, *kidnap* means to abduct either a child or an adult.

A kid is a young goat, and that is the origin of the word's slang use for a child.

"Kidding around" is acting childish.

What is the origin of the word *tip*, as in "tipping a waiter"?

Tip is not an acronym for "To Insure Promptness." In the 1800s a tip was understood to be a bribe. As insider information, *tip* first appeared in the seventeenth century and derives from the Low German word *tippen*, which means "to touch discreetly." A tip is something confidential, whether given or received — either from a stockbroker or to a waiter.

Why are both a published periodical and a place to house ammunition called a "magazine"?

The word *magazine* is from the Arabic word *makhzan*, meaning "a place to store arms and ammunition." The word entered English to describe a munitions warehouse or the chamber that holds bullets in a loaded gun.

In 1731, the word took on its new meaning with the publication of *The Gentlemen's Magazine*, so called because it held an assortment of articles of different shapes and sizes.

Why are men who work on the docks called "longshoremen"?

The title *longshoreman* goes back to a time when there was very little mechanical help to unload a great sailing vessel, and often there were no port or docking facilities either. Everything was done by hand. Unloading the big ship into smaller rowing boats, then unloading these onto the shore, was hard work and needed a lot of strong men. Because these men would line up on the water's edge, they were called "along the shore men" which in time became simply "longshoremen."

Why are young women and girlfriends sometimes referred to as "birds"?

Referring to young women as birds dates back to the Anglo-Saxons, who used the endearment *brid*, meaning "baby animal." *Brid* is the

derivative of *bride*, and over time, the term created a number of similar words, all of them having to do with young women. During the 1920s, the flapper look was named after a baby duck. The cancan, popular in France in the 1890s, took its name from *canard*, which is French for duck. When they danced, the girls displayed their tail feathers. The original dancers wore no underwear.

The computer terms *byte*, *pixel*, and *modem* are abbreviations of what combinations of words?

Each word is a contraction of two words. *Byte* is a contraction of the words *by eight* and means eight bits. Half a byte is four bits (or a nibble, depending how you look at it). The word *pixel* is an abbreviation of *picture cell*, while *modem* is a combination of the first letters in the words *modulate* and *demodulate*.

Why does *long* mean length, distance, and an emotion?

Longing for someone evolved from *long*, as in length, around 1000 AD. Around 1300 AD, *long* began to define a period of time because it seemed forever for someone to travel a great distance when a donkey cart was rapid transit. In this day of jet travel, yearning or longing for someone who is far away isn't the same, because you can always call long distance.

Why is the entrance to a house called a "threshold"?

Today, crossing the threshold signifies a figurative beginning, but a thousand years ago, a threshold was just the floorboard in the doorway of a country cottage. *Threshing* is the process of separating wheat from the straw. While the wheat was stored, straw, among other things, was used to cover both slate and dirt floors. The board in the doorway that held the straw inside was called the *threshold* — holder of the straw.

What do the words *hunky-dory* and *honcho* have in common?

If everything is great then it's *hunky-dory*, while a *honcho* is a big shot, and both words come from Japan. During the First World War, American sailors on leave discovered a Yokohama street named Huncho-dori that provided all the facilities for carnal pleasure. They brought home the name and the good feeling as *hunky-dory*. *Honcho* came out of the Second World War and is Japanese for "squad leader."

Where did the word *gimmick* come from?

Gimmick or *gimac* — either way it's spelled, a *gimmick* is a gadget or idea that gives you an advantage. The second spelling is an anagram of *magic*; the word comes from the language of professional magicians and means a small, secret device, like a mirror or sliding panel, that makes an illusion possible. Carnival barkers picked up *gimac* in the 1920s as a reference to a hidden control over their wheels of chance that ensured the wheel would stop when the barkers wanted it to stop. Today, a gimmick is most often used in advertising or selling, but it's still part of an illusion.

Why are slaves to substance abuse called "addicts"?

After the Romans conquered most of Slavonia, the word *Slav* became synonymous with subjugated people. *Slav* gave us the word *slave*. Slavs were given as rewards to Roman warriors and were known by the Latin word for slaves — *addicts*. If your life is controlled by anything other than your own will, you are a slave to those circumstances. Eventually a person who was a slave to anything was called an addict.

What does *whelm* mean in *overwhelmed*?

An author facing writer's block is overwhelmed by indecision. The word started out in the 1300s as *whelm*, meaning to overturn or cover.

For example, food was preserved by whelming it with another dish, or a capsized ship had been whelmed by the ocean. In the 1600s, *over* was added to intensify the meaning. *Overwhelm* then became figurative for being drowned by circumstances.

What's the purpose of a catchword?

Catchword is from the world of print. Two hundred years ago, the last word on a page to be turned began being routinely repeated at the top of the next page to smooth the transition. Newspapers followed by repeating the last word of an article when it was picked up deeper into the paper. In the theatre, a catchword is the cue for the next actor to start his lines. A catchphrase is a political or commercial slogan.

The first use of catchwords in a printed book was *Tacitus*, by John de Spira (1469).

If someone fails to perform under pressure, why do we say he "choked"?

To choke is to restrict airflow, whether to human lungs or the carburetor of a car. In ancient times, the guilt or innocence of an accused robber was established by making him swallow a piece of barley bread over which a Mass had been said. He had to do this while repeating words from that Mass. If he swallowed without choking, he was innocent, but if he choked he was pronounced guilty. This gave us the expression "choking under pressure."

Legend has it that the Earl of Godwin died while choking on a piece of bread during this legal process.

What does *monger* mean in words like *hate-monger* or *gossipmonger*?

There are gossipmongers, warmongers, scandal-mongers, hate-mongers, and many others to whom we show extreme disrespect by adding the perceived curse *monger* to their action; yet when the word stands alone it isn't that severe. From the old English word *mangian*, *mong* simply means "to peddle, sell, or barter," so a fishmonger sells fish, while a hate-monger peddles hate.

EXPRESSIONS

Where do we get the saying "Think outside the box"?

The phrase is an allusion to a well-known puzzle where one has to connect nine dots, arranged in a square grid, with four straight lines drawn continuously without pen leaving paper. The only solution to this puzzle is one where some of the lines extend beyond the border of the grid (or box). This puzzle was a popular gimmick among management consultants in the 1970s and '80s as a demonstration of the need to discard unwarranted assumptions (like the assumption that the lines must remain within the grid).

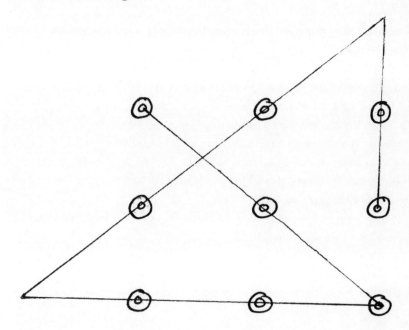

If we want the truth, why do we say, "Read between the lines"?

Sometimes the truth is obscured within the written text of a letter, and so we must "read between the lines." Centuries ago it was discovered that by writing a secret message between the lines of a normal letter with lemon juice, the real message would stay transparent until the document was heated over a flame, which causes the juice to become discoloured, revealing the intended message written between the lines of the ruse.

If your reputation is ruined, why is your name mud?

After John Wilkes Booth assassinated President Lincoln at the Ford Theatre, he broke his leg while leaping from the balcony and onto the stage. During his escape, Booth stopped in at the home of a country doctor for treatment. That doctor's name was Mudd. Although he claimed no knowledge of Booth's crime, Dr. Mudd was sent to prison, and in America, his name became unfairly synonymous with disrepute.

If someone's running from punishment, why do we say he's "on the lam"?

Being "on the lam" means to be on the run and became popular in the American underworld near the end of the nineteenth century. *Lam* is from the Viking word *lamja* meaning "to make lame" and was used in England during the sixteenth century as "a sound beating." The words *lame* and *lambaste* are related. If someone hit the road because staying would result in severe punishment, they were "on the lam" or on the list for a beating (or worse).

Baste is from a Nordic word meaning "thrash" or "flog," so *lambaste* is an even more severe beating.

If people hide their past, why do we say they have "skeletons in their closets"?

The expression about skeletons in a closet comes from a fairy tale about Bluebeard the pirate, who, legend has it, murdered all his many wives. When he gave his new wife the keys to the house, he forbade her to open a specific closet at the end of a long hall — which, of course, she did the moment he left on business. When she unlocked the door and looked inside, she was horrified to find all the skeletons of Bluebeard's previous wives.

Why, under urgent circumstances, do we say we have to "strike while the iron is hot"?

To strike while the iron is hot means to act quickly before an opportunity is gone. In medieval Europe, blacksmiths worked red-hot iron by hand from a forge. They shaped the heated metal with a hammer before it cooled, so they needed to work quickly, because as the iron cools it becomes brittle and impossible to work with. If the moment is missed, the metal has to be reheated and the process started over.

Why do we say that someone who is sharp is "on the ball?

To be "on the ball" means to be at the top of your game. We have all heard a pitcher's excuse of not having his "stuff" after a bad outing and wondered how that excuse would work with our bosses if we had a bad day. From the early days of baseball, when a pitcher couldn't find the spin and lost control, it's been said he had "nothing on the ball" which gave us "on the ball" as meaning "he's in control."

Why do we say that someone in control has "the upper hand"?

Someone with the "upper hand" has the final say over a situation. When a group of youngsters gather to pick sides at a game of sandlot baseball, the two captains decide who chooses first when one of them grasps the bat at the bottom of the handle. The captains take turns gripping the bat one fist over the other until there was no more room. The last one to fully grip the bat handle has first choice. He has the upper hand.

Why do we say, "Take a powder" when we want someone to leave?

"Take a powder" is a tough way of telling someone to get lost or get out of here and began as a rude dismissal of women. It was popularized in the gangster movies of the 1930s; when a tough guy was having a private conversation that he didn't want a woman to overhear, he would use the phrase that the girls used when they excused themselves to use the washroom or refresh their makeup. They'd say they were "taking a powder."

Why do we say that something flawed "isn't all it's cracked up to be"?

If something isn't all it was cracked up to be, then it's less than advertised, it's a disappointment. *Crack* began as the verb "to praise or boast" in the fifteenth century and today is often used as a noun. For example, you might be cracked up by a good wisecrack. In the South, a cracker is a feeble-minded braggart. And if you've lost it, you've gone crackers. No matter how you look at it, if it isn't all it's cracked up to be, you've been had.

Why is a swindle called a "double-cross"?

If you cross someone, you're cheating him. A double-cross means you are cheating both your employer and the one you've been hired to deceive. In the 1800s, Thackeray described a fixed horse race in *Vanity Fair* where the jockey who was prearranged to lose was instead allowed to win, costing the gamblers a fortune. Because the fixer had crossed or cheated both parties for a huge profit, the win was called a "double-cross."

Why is an alley with only one exit or entrance called a "blind alley"?

Have you ever heard the Biblical quotation about how a rich man's chances of getting to heaven are about the same as a camel passing through the eye of a needle? An eye is an ancient reference to an opening in a wall or a gate, because you could see through it. If there is an obstruction (or in the case of the alley, a wall), then there is no "eye" to see or escape through — it is a blind alley.

Why do we describe an upset person as being "beside himself"?

If someone is beside himself, he is extremely distraught. You might even say he is out of his mind, because the ancients believed that under extreme distress the soul left a man's body and stood beside the human form, which left the subject literally "beside himself." This absence of the soul gave the Devil an opportunity to fill the void. Extreme pleasure could also cause this condition. The Greek word *ecstasy* means "to stand out of the body."

What's the story behind the expression "It's a dog-eat-dog world"?

In the year 43 BC, Roman scholar Marcus Tarentius Varro observed humanity and remarked that even "a dog will not eat dog." His point was that humans are less principled in the matter of destroying their own

kind than other animals. By the sixteenth century, the phrase became a metaphor for ruthless competition, and during the Industrial Revolution the expression "It's a dog-eat-dog world" became commonplace.

Why, if you're insincere, do we say you're "talking through your hat"?

Saying something without conviction might be called a lie, or you could be accused of "talking through your hat." Around 1850, an Englishman refused to kneel before sitting in a church pew, a serious breach of religious etiquette. Instead, he whispered a prayer while covering his mouth with his hat before sitting down. This shocked the other worshippers, and although many copied him, "Talking through your hat" took on the meaning of false and irreverent.

Why do we say that something very obvious is "as clear as a bell"?

In a simpler time when birds could be heard above traffic or construction noise, a single clear note sounded by a church bell could be heard over a wide area and was used to communicate time, to announce a celebration or important event, or even to warn of an impending attack. When the bell sounded, everyone heard the message as clear as a bell.

Why do we call the conclusion of anything unpleasant "the bitter end"?

"The bitter end" has been used to describe the conclusion of something distasteful since the mid-nineteenth century. It's a play on the word *bitter*, as in "sour," and the nautical *bitters*, the posts on a ships deck where cables and ropes are wound and tied. When securing the ship to the dock, or while at anchor, the very end of the rope or cable holding the vessel secure is called the bitter end.

Why are unrealistic fantasies called "pipe dreams"?

Pipe dreams are often schemes that just won't work. Like daydreams, pipe dreams dissolve like smoke rising into the air — which is appropriate, because the metaphor comes from smoking opium. It can be traced to print in the late nineteenth century, when it was fashionable for hedonists and the upper classes to escape reality through an opium pipe. Those "on the pipe" were experiencing opium-induced "pipe dreams."

Why does "to bear the brunt" mean "to take the heat"?

"To take the heat" is the literal translation of "to bear the brunt," because *brunt* and *burn* mean the same thing. From the Anglo-Saxon word *brenning*, or *burning*, *brunt* was a vivid reference to the hottest point of conflict during a battle. It took on a more general meaning to describe contentious domestic and business issues, but it always means the utmost pressure within a circumstance, or the point of greatest fury.

What are the meaning and the origin of the expression "The be-all and end-all"?

Shakespeare introduced the expression, meaning "the ultimate or most important solution," as dialogue for Macbeth, who thinks about killing Duncan and wonders "that this blow might be the be-all and the end-all" (*MacBeth* I vii. IV). Macbeth then says he would risk his status in the afterlife if it were true. Today, Shakespeare's second "the" is usually dropped but "the be-all and end-all" still means "the ultimate."

How did the expression "dead as a doornail" originate?

When metal nails were introduced to construction, they were hand tooled, which made them very rare and equally expensive. When an aging house or barn with metal nails was torn down it was important to collect and reuse the nails. Because previous carpenters had bent the sharp end of the doornails for safety and to stabilize them against constant opening and closing, they were useless for recycling, which made them "dead."

Where did the expression "I've got to see a man about a dog" originate?

It's the room we most often frequent, but good manners dictate that we avoid direct references to the toilet at all costs. It's a restroom, a powder room, a washroom, and a loo, which is derived from the French word *l'eau* for water, as in water closet. "Seeing a man about a dog" comes from the 1866 play *Flying Scud* where a character says, "Excuse me Mr. Quail, I can't stop; I've got to see a man about a dog" meaning he needs to leave the room — and fast.

Flying Scud was written by Irish-born playwright Dion Boucicault.

If someone lacks confidence, why do we say that he's "selling himself short"?

If someone sells himself short, he's probably nervous about the future, and for good reason. The expression comes from the stock market. "Selling short" means that you're selling shares you don't yet own. If an investor believes a stock is on the decline, he might gamble by selling it before purchasing it in the future at a lower price. The difference is his profit; unless the stock goes down, he pays the consequences of selling short.

What does it mean to be footloose and fancy-free?

To be footloose and fancy-free means to be free from any responsibilities, or in other words, to be single. The expression started appearing in print around 1700 with *footloose* simply meaning your ankles were unshackled so you could go anywhere you wanted. *Fancy* was a sixteenth-century word for being attracted to someone of the opposite sex. If you weren't in love, you were "fancy-free."

What's the origin of the expression "Put on your thinking cap"?

Teachers will often tell students to "put on their thinking caps" when they want them to take time to think things over. Caps have been associated with academics, jurists, scholars, and clerics for centuries. One of the most familiar of these caps is the mortarboard worn at graduation, so called for its similarity to the instrument used by bricklayers. In the seventeenth century, English judges wore a "considering cap" while pondering a sentence.

Why, when abbreviating something, do we say, "In a nutshell"?

"In a nutshell" indicates a drastically reduced summary. Long before modern electronics, a few scholars made attempts at condensing massive literary works so they could be more easily stored. It became an obsession to some to see just how small they could write. For example, a copy of the Qur'an was reduced on a parchment measuring four inches by half an inch. These copies were so small it was said they could be stored in a nutshell.

What do I mean by saying, "If I had my druthers"?

"If had my druthers" means, of course, "If I had my way." *Druthers* is always plural and indicates that there are a number of options other than what is offered. It's rural American slang; it began as "I'd rather," which, when shortened by dropping the "I" becomes "drather." With a country accent, "drather" becomes "druther," which when pluralized and extended becomes "druthers" meaning "choices."

When being dismissive, why do we say, "Go fly a kite"?

Flying a kite is a good way to see which way the wind is blowing. In the nineteenth century, when a man was looking for employment or searching for investors, he would send out letters to strangers in much the same way as people send out resumes today. "Go fly a kite" meant "I can't help you, but keep sending out those letters."

Why do "guts" and "pluck" mean courage?

Having "guts" or "pluck" means having courage or backbone, while having neither means lily-livered cowardice, and they are all references to intestinal fortitude. *Guts*, of course, are internal organs while *pluck* is collectively the heart, liver, and lungs. *Lily-livered* comes from the belief that fear drains blood from the liver, making it white. It was once believed that these internal organs, specifically the heart, were the source of a person's character.

In the eighteenth century, the pluck contained the heart, liver, lights, melt, and skirt (lights were lungs, melt was the collected blood, and the skirt was the diaphragm).

CHILDHOOD

What is the origin of the children's rhyme "Eeney, meeney, miney, moe"?

"Eeney, meeney, miney, moe" is a children's rhyme where, with each word, the person counting or reciting points at one of a group of players to establish who will be "it." The ritual was handed down from the Druids, who used the same counting formula to choose human sacrifices. The precise meanings and origins of the words *eeney, meeney, miney* and *moe* are unknown. The theory that the rhyme is from an ancient Anglo-Saxon, Celtic, or Welsh numbering system can't be proven.

The rhyme was first written down in 1855 along with several other versions, for example, "Hanna, mana, mona, mike."

Why is rolling head over heels called a "somersault"?

A somersault is a stunt in which a person tumbles head over heels; it can be very difficult, as when performed by a circus acrobat, or very simple, as when performed by a child on a front lawn. The word has two Latin derivatives, *supra*, meaning above and *saltus*, meaning "leap." It entered England from France as *sombresault*. One of the word's alternate spellings was used to name the English county of Somerset.

The word *somersault* first appeared in English around 1530 as *sobersault*, and by the nineteenth century it was *sumersault*.

What are the origins of the merry-go-round?

When medieval noblemen were looking for a sport to replace their brutal jousting tournaments, they turned to a training exercise of catching rings from horseback, known in Spanish as *carossela*, meaning "little war." *Carossela* gave us *carousel*. In time, live horses were replaced with hanging revolving seats, which in turn gave way to painted wooden horses, and from this evolved the merry-go-round.

Where did the game hopscotch come from?

Hopscotch was brought to Britain by the Romans, who used it as a military training exercise. The courts were one hundred feet long, and the soldiers ran them in full battle gear to improve their footwork. Children copied the soldiers by scratching out small courses of their own and creating rules and a scoring system. The *scotch* in *hopscotch* refers to the markings scored onto the ground. As in butterscotch toffee, *scotch* means scored or notched into squares.

What's the origin of the phrase "goody two-shoes"?

A "goody two-shoes" is an unbearably self-centred little girl and comes from a nursery rhyme, "The History of Little Goody Two-shoes." "Goody" was a common nickname for married women and came from the word *goodwife*. In the nursery rhyme, Goody owned only one shoe. When given a pair, she ran around showing them to everyone, even those less fortunate than she, smugly announcing, "Look! Two shoes." The phrase came to mean a self-centred brat.

"The History of Little Goody Two-shoes," inspired by an actual person, was written by Oliver Goldsmith and published in 1765 by John Newberry. The real Goody's full name was Margery Meanwell, and she lived in Mouldwell.

"Twinkle, Twinkle Little Star" shares a melody with three other nursery rhymes, but which two classical composers also used the melody?

In 1806, Jane Taylor published "Twinkle, Twinkle Little Star" simply as "The Star." The tune was already in use for "Baa Baa Black Sheep" and the Alphabet Song. The melody for all three came from a French rhyme called "Ah! Vous dirais-je Maman" (1765). Both Mozart and Haydn have incorporated the melody into two of their classical compositions: Haydn in "Surprise" Symphony No.94 and Mozart in Theme and Variations K265.

Why does the childhood word *dibs* mean "It's mine"?

To put "dibs" on something, like a piece of cake (or Dad's car), is to express first claim to a share of that object. The word dates from before 1700 and comes from a very old children's game called *dib-stone*, a forerunner to marbles, which was played with either sheep knuckles or small stones. The object was to capture an opponent's stone by declaring, "I dibs!" meaning, "It's mine!" The plural of the word was *dubs*.

Why when lifting a young child, might you say, "Ups-a-daisy"?

Whether it's "Ups-a-daisy," "Whoops-a-daisy," or "Oops-a-daisy," you are speaking loving nonsense, usually to a child. "Up-a-dazy" dates back to 1711, and by 1862 it had mutated into "Up-a-daisy," spelled the same as the flower. The original meaning was an encouragement for a child to get up, and *dazy* was an endearing reference to *lazy*, an abbreviation of *lackadaisical*.

What's the meaning behind "Pop Goes the Weasel"?

The old song, with every verse ending in "Pop goes the weasel," is a tale of Victorian London working-class poverty. The Eagle of the lyrics was a famous pub. The City Road still exists. "Pop" means to pawn something for cash, while a "weasel" in cockney rhyming slang is a coat. After spending his money on rice and treacle, followed by a visit to the pub, the man in the song is forced to visit the pawnshop for more money — thus selling his belongings, or "Pop goes the weasel."

TRIVIA

How did the Swedish company IKEA get its name?

Born in 1926 in the Swedish village of Agunnaryd, Ingvar Kamprad got his start by riding his bicycle from farm to farm selling wooden matches. Once everyone had a supply of matches, Ingvar wisely decided to diversify his offerings and soon was pedaling around the countryside delivering Christmas tree ornaments, ballpoint pens, and, though it must have been a bit awkward, fresh fish. By age seventeen, Ingvar had formed his own company and named it IKEA, an acronym made up of his own initials, the name of his family's farm (Elmtaryd), and the village of his birth.

Delivering his products (which now included picture frames, watches, and jewellery) by bicycle was no longer practical, so Ingvar transformed IKEA into a mail-order operation; by 1948 he was also selling furniture produced by local artisans. So successful was his low-priced but sturdy furniture that by 1951 he had dropped all his other products and decided to concentrate on inexpensive but stylish home furnishings.

What is the chief difference between a limited company (Ltd.) and one that's incorporated (Inc.)?

A company name ending in *Ltd.* means that the amount of risk or liability for its shareholders for any corporate failure or debt is limited to the amount of their personal investment in that company. In an incorporated company or corporation (*Inc.*), the business is recognized as a single entity, and the personal assets of its principals are protected from creditors if the business fails. Only stockholders risk losing the amount of their investment.

Why is something or someone of superior quality called "a cut above"?

"A cut above" dates from the eighteenth century and literally means the quality of the cutting or fashioning of a person's clothing. The superior appearance or station in life of someone with a good tailor or milliner is obvious when compared with a common man or woman, making them a "cut above" the ordinary. The phrase is related to the nautical phrase "The cut of her jib," meaning the style or cut of a ship's sails. You can also be a "cut below," as in "The girl herself is a cut below par" (A.B. Walford, 1891).

Why is it bad luck to whistle backstage in a theatre?

Whistling backstage became bad luck during a time in England when stagehands were most often sailors without a ship. The curtain, flies, and props were moved manually by a system of ropes, so the sailors communicated as they did at sea: by whistling. If someone not involved in the intricate backstage manoeuvres were to whistle, a stagehand might take it as a cue, which could be disastrous for the production.

What was the original meaning of "stem the tide"?

The general (yet incorrect) use of "stem the tide" is to deflect a serious problem, but tides can't be deflected. A *stem* is the upright beam at the fore of the ship where the hull timbers form the prow. The nautical manoeuvre against a surging tide is the same as against an angry sea. The ship is turned to stem the onslaught. To "stem the tide" means that to overcome serious problems, you must face them head-on.

What is the origin of the thimble?

A thimble is more than a token in a Monopoly game. Its true name is *thumb-bell*, and before the seventeenth century, when it was invented in Holland, pushing a sewing needle through skins or fabric often required the use of a small block of wood or bone. Thimbles have a romantic history, and during the Victorian era thimbles were often love tokens. They were even used to measure drinks, which gave us the expression, "Just a thimble-full."

A person who collects thimbles is a digitabulist.

Why does "XXX" warn us about sexually explicit material?

The first use of the X brand was on casks of English beer and indicated that the contents had been properly aged and had passed government approval after paying a ten-shilling duty, illustrated by the Roman numeral X. Some brewers added extra Xs to suggest a more potent content, and smut peddlers followed suit. When something is X-rated by the censors, its naughtiness is enhanced if more Xs are added.

Why are the contorted faces and heads around roofs called "gargoyles"?

Ancient Celtic warriors used to place the severed heads of their enemies around the top of their fortresses as a warning. In time these inspired architects to add the twisted faces of gargoyles to prominent buildings. Gargoyles had the practical purpose of collecting rainwater and dropping it clear of the walls through their throats. In ancient French, *gargouille* means "throat."

Why do doors generally open inward on a house and outward on public buildings?

Doors generally open outward on public buildings as a precaution against fire. If dozens of people have to rush for the exit, they won't have to fight to pull the door inward against the crush. The exceptions are those institutions fearing robbery, which have doors opening inward to delay the getaway and, like the doors of your home, to keep the hinges on the inside so that burglars can't simply remove the door.

On a standard computer or typewriter, which hand controls the most keys?

When a typists hands take the standard position taught around the world, the left hand controls fifteen letters, including the most frequently used, E, A, T, R and S, while the right hand controls only eleven, although it also controls the comma and the period. The left hand makes about 56 percent of the strokes leaving 44 percent for the right. *Reverberates*, *effervesce*, and *stewardess* can be typed entirely with the left hand. *Monopoly*, *homonym*, and *lollipop* can be typed using only the right hand. The delete/backspace keys come under the right, which equalizes the workload between the two hands for an average typist.

QUESTION LIST

Travel & Distance

Politics & the Law

War & the Military

Holidays

YOUR QUESTIONS AND ANSWERS

If you have a question and haven't found the answer in my first three volumes of *Now You Know, The Book of Answers*, I would like to find that answer for you.

Likewise, if you have an interesting answer or information within our format that hasn't already been included in volumes 1, 2, or 3, please send it to me by regular mail to:

Now You Know c/o Dundurn Press, 3 Church Street, Suite 500, Toronto, Ontario, Canada, M5E 1M2 or via email directly to dlennoxc593@rogers.com

We will credit your name and hometown if your question or answer is used in a future volume.